SAINTS BEYOND
THE WHITE
CLIFFS

SAINT THOMAS BECKET FACES THE KNIGHTS (*page* 159)

SAINTS BEYOND THE WHITE CLIFFS

STORIES OF ENGLISH SAINTS

By

MARGARET GIBBS

Illustrated by
T. H. ROBINSON

Biography Index Reprint Series

BOOKS FOR LIBRARIES PRESS
FREEPORT, NEW YORK

First Published 1947

Reprinted 1971 by arrangement with
Miss M. Gibbs and her literary agents, A. P. Watt and Son

Illustrations reproduced by arrangement with
Hollis & Carter Ltd.

INTERNATIONAL STANDARD BOOK NUMBER:
0-8369-8058-1

LIBRARY OF CONGRESS CATALOG CARD NUMBER:
75-148211

PRINTED IN THE UNITED STATES OF AMERICA

DATES OF SAINTS

SAINT GEORGE	Fourth Century
SAINT ALBAN	Died 304
SAINT ETHELBERT OF KENT	„ 616
SAINT HILDA	„ 680
SAINT MILDRED	„ 700
SAINT WILFRID	„ 709
SAINT GUTHLAC	„ 714
SAINT FRIDESWIDE	„ 735
SAINT DUNSTAN	„ 988
SAINT GODRIC	„ 1170
SAINT THOMAS BECKET	„ 1170
SAINT HUGH OF LINCOLN	„ 1200
SAINT RICHARD OF CHICHESTER	„ 1253

CONTENTS

Page

They tried to make him say that what he had cried out was not true.

I

SAINT GEORGE—PROTECTOR OF ENGLAND

The Emperor's Decree

EVERYONE in England has heard of Saint George and the Dragon. Not so many know who Saint George really was, and what he did. It is not a long story, but it tells how Saint George did something even braver than dragon slaying.

This is what happened :

George was a Christian knight who lived in Cappadocia. Cappadocia was a part of Asia Minor, and Asia Minor was a part of the Roman Empire. This was in the fourth century, when Diocletian was Emperor of Rome.

Now, at that time, Christianity was spreading quickly. More and more people were deciding to be Christians, not only the poor and unimportant ones, but great lords and ladies, soldiers and princes. They did not have to hide in catacombs and places, but worshipped God openly in their own churches. However, there were still plenty of pagans left, including the Emperor Diocletian, and a man named Galerius who was his heir ; and the pagans (especially Galerius) simply hated the Christians and were only waiting for a chance to destroy them utterly.

At last it came. A rumour went round that there was a plot against Galerius, and that some of the Christians were in it.

"Ah-ha !" exclaimed Galerius, "*Now* we've got them !"

I

As luck would have it, he was just going to the city of Nicomedia to see the Emperor, and he seized the opportunity to persuade Diocletian to crush the Christians.

Suddenly, without warning—it happened ! One morning the Royal Guard appeared before the Cathedral in Nicomedia, broke open the doors, and rushed in. They turned the whole place upside down, destroyed everything they came upon, burnt all the books of the Scriptures and then destroyed the Cathedral itself.

Next day a great notice was fastened up in the centre of the city. It said that all the Christian churches were to be destroyed and the Scriptures burnt. Nobody was to dare to be a Christian any longer : if they did, they would not count as citizens any more, and if they held some high rank, such as Lord or General, they would lose it. And all this was By Order of the Emperor.

It was a terrible surprise for the Christians, because everything had been going on so nicely until then. They were quite dazed, and rather frightened, for to tell you the truth, though they all wanted very much to be Christians, they did *not* want to be martyrs. Most of them were just ordinary people like ourselves, not specially brave, and when they started being Christians it had seemed perfectly safe. But now, they asked each other—now, what would happen ?

What might have happened, if they had all been afraid and given in, is that Christianity might have been stamped out—at least for a time.

However, luckily, there was Saint George.

Saint George—of course he was not " Saint " then, but just ordinary George—came into Nicomedia feeling rather worried because he had heard rumours of what was happening, and he was afraid the Christians *might* give in if things were very difficult. The first thing he saw when he entered the city was that notice. He could scarcely believe his eyes ! Without a moment's hesitation he rushed at it, tore it down, screwed it into a ball and threw it away! Then he shouted at the top of his voice:

"All the gods of the pagans are devils! My God is the *real* God!"

He could not have chosen a worse time to do such a thing, for both Diocletian and Galerius were in the city, and it was like defying both at once. Not that that would have stopped George from standing up for Christianity!

He was instantly arrested, carried off to prison, and tortured. They tried to make him say that what he had cried out in the Square was not true, but he would not. They tried to make him stop being a Christian, but he would not. They tortured and tortured him, and it was terrible, but he would not give in. So at last they killed him, and he became Saint George the Martyr.

After his death the Christians had a dreadful time and a great many more of them were martyrs. But in the end they won, and their children and grandchildren were able to be Christians without being martyrs as well.

But they might have lost, if it had not been for Saint George.

The Dragon of Silene

LONG after he was dead, Saint George and his great deed were remembered, and as time went on all kinds of legends grew up of other mighty deeds which he was supposed to have done. The best of these is the one about the dragon, and this is how it goes:

There was once a town called Silene, ruled over by a King who had one fair daughter.

Now, the people of Silene went in great terror and distress because of a fearful dragon that lived near by. It lurked in a pond outside the city walls, and every day it would arise from the waters in search of food. So fearful was this creature that even its breath was poisonous, and the people were in constant fear that it would attack the city.

At last the King hit upon a plan to keep the monster at bay.

" If we can keep it well fed," said he, " it will probably do us no harm. We must arrange to leave food for it beside the pond each day. That should keep it quiet, at least. And you don't know—it might even grow quite tame—in time."

And so it was arranged. Every day the people drew lots to see whose turn it was to provide the dragon's dinner. They began with sheep ; when they were all gone, they used pigs, goats, calves and even poultry. So long as these lasted all was well, and the people were very pleased. But at last these, too, were all eaten. There was nothing left at all on which to feed the dragon.

The King was in despair. The people cowered in their houses, asking themselves what would happen next.

It must, I think, have been a man with no children of his own : with no nieces and nephews, or grandchildren, or little-boys-next-door, who made the next suggestion. It was this : Since the sheep and pigs and poultry were all gone—*what about starting on the children ?*

" The children ? " At first the people just whispered the words, scarcely daring to think what was really being suggested. But at last, when they could bear the roaring of the hungry dragon no longer, they spoke them aloud.

" Suppose we feed the dragon on children ? "

And that was what they did. They drew lots, as before, to see which child should go, and each morning a boy or girl was left beside the pond.

I don't think I like the people of Silene very much.

Now, if you remember, the King himself had one fair daughter, and at last it came to her turn to go to the dragon.

The King was furious.

" Do you dare to suggest that *my* daughter should be given to this monster ? " he demanded.

" Certainly, Your Majesty," replied his Counsellors, respectfully, but firmly.

" Of course I must go, Father," put in the Princess. " It wouldn't be fair to the others if I didn't."

So the people of Silene thought, and so, the very next morning, the Princess was led out to her fate, dressed as a bride, and looking even lovelier than usual. Great crowds followed her to the spot, weeping as they went, for they loved her dearly.

But the Princess did not weep. She walked proudly and firmly, holding her head high, so that no one should guess she was afraid.

At last they came to the marsh which surrounded the dragon's pond. There they left her, and went sorrowfully homeward.

The Princess looked at the pond, and shivered. Then she began to cry. There was no one to see her now, so it did not matter : she just cried and cried.

All at once a voice spoke, close beside her :

" Is anything the matter ? "

The Princess looked up with a start. Beside her stood a splendid great horse, and upon his back sat a tall young knight, looking down at her with the kindest expression.

" What is the matter, Lady ? " he asked. " What makes you weep so bitterly ? "

The Princess shook her head.

" It's nothing," she answered. " At least—nothing that can be helped. Please go on your way, and don't worry about me."

" But I can't leave you here like this ! " exclaimed the Knight (who of course was Saint George). " Alone, and in trouble ! Won't you tell me what is wrong ? It may be that it *can* be helped, after all."

The Princess stopped crying, and looked gravely at Saint George. He had so kind and so friendly a look, and she was so terribly sad and frightened and lonely, that at last she took heart and told him all about the dragon.

When he heard the tale, the eyes of Saint George flashed like his sword.

" What ! " he cried. " Were there none in all the city

who would do battle with this monster ? Are they all cowards in Silene ? ”

“ Oh! no,” the Princess assured him hastily. “ They’re very nice people—really they are. Only he is such a terrible dragon. *Anyone* would be afraid of him.”

“ Ha ! ” snorted Saint George. “ We shall see about that ! ”

At that very moment, there was a great heaving and splashing from the middle of the pond.

“ Oh ! he’s coming ! ” screamed the Princess. “ Oh ! do go. Please, please go ! ”

But instead of going, Saint George settled himself more firmly in his saddle, and drew his sword.

“ Don’t be afraid, Princess,” he said, giving her a nice, encouraging smile, and as he spoke, the dragon rose up out of the pond.

Then began the most terrific fight. The dragon raged and roared, lashing his great tail, snapping and snarling and breathing fire and poison, but Saint George was more than a match for him. At last, after a fearful battle, he struck one mighty blow, and the dragon sank down with a moan.

“ Is he dead ? ” called the Princess, who had watched the battle with a fast-beating heart.

“ Not quite,” answered Saint George, “ but he won’t hurt you. Come and see.”

The Princess went gingerly forward. “ Oh ! how can I possibly thank you properly ? ” she exclaimed, when she saw the monster lying at her feet.

“ It is nothing,” said Saint George. “ A Knight must always defend a lady. See, the creature is quite harmless now. Lend me your girdle, will you ? I’ll tie it round his neck—so. There ! Now we will take him to the town and show him to the people.”

But the Princess said :

“ Shall I not lead him myself ? When the townsfolk see the mighty dragon led captive by a maiden, they will know that he is harmless indeed.”

And thus they entered the town—the Princess leading the dragon like a dog on a leash. But even then the people, when they caught sight of him, began to run away.

"Come back, come back!" cried Saint George. "There is no danger. The dragon is beaten. See, he allows the Princess to lead him by her girdle."

When at last the people understood what had happened, a huge crowd gathered in the Square to see the monster. Presently, there was a shout of "Make way there!" The crowd parted, and the King came through, followed by his Counsellors.

–"Father, dear Father!" cried the Princess, running to the King, and flinging her arms about his neck.

"But what has happened, my dear?" asked the King, quite bewildered.

"I have been saved by this gallant Knight," answered the Princess. Then, standing up before them all, she told how Saint George had vanquished the dragon and saved her and all the city.

There were loud cheers for Saint George when the story was ended. When they had died down, the King said:

"This was truly a gallant deed. But would it not be safer if the dragon were actually dead?"

Then Saint George had a good idea.

"Listen," said he. "If you will all become Christians, I will slay the dragon for you."

The King considered.

"Could you explain to us about Christianity first?" he asked.

"Gladly," replied Saint George, and he did. And the people liked what he told them so much that then and there they all decided to be Christians.

Thereupon, Saint George lifted his great sword, and slew the dragon with one blow.

"And now," said he, "I must go, for there are many other wrongs in the world to be righted."

But the King cried:

" Stay ! Before you go, pray accept this reward," and he offered Saint George a bag of treasure.

But Saint George waved it away.

" Please give it to the poor folk of the city," said he. " I'm sure they need it much more than I do."

" But you must have a reward," insisted the King.

" Well," said Saint George, after a moment. " There is something you can do, if you will, as a Thanksgiving to God for sending me to slay the dragon for you."

" Only tell us," said the King. " We will do anything you say." And the people clapped to show that they agreed.

" Then promise me," said Saint George, "that you will do these four things :

> Look after the Churches properly.
> Honour the priests.
> Go to church regularly.
> Be kind and helpful to poor people."

Solemnly, the King and his people promised.

Then Saint George rode away, and was seen in that city no more.

.   .   .   .   .

But how does it happen that Saint George is Patron Saint of England ?

Well, that was largely through the Crusades. Crusaders, coming home from fighting in the Holy Land, brought tales of how Saint George had appeared to them in visions, and how twice, when things were going very badly for them, and it seemed as if they must lose the battle, he had come and helped them and they had won after all. So the Crusaders began to feel that Saint George took a particular interest in them, and naturally that made them take a particular interest in him. They took " St. George ! " for their battle cry, and they always felt sure he was with them.

But the story goes that it was the English soldiers who

went with King Richard the Lion Heart to the Holy Land who first thought of having Saint George for our Patron Saint.

They were fond of telling stories round their camp fires, these English soldiers, and the tale that everyone liked best was the one about Saint George and the Dragon. And so, one night, when the story had been told for the hundredth time, one of the soldiers had an idea. He suggested that they should ask the King if they might have Saint George for Patron Saint of England. And so he has been ever since.

I think it was a very fine idea—don't you?

Alban snatched up the old man's cloak.

II

SAINT ALBAN—THE FRIEND
IN NEED

HEN the Romans ruled in Britain they built a city on the banks of the River Ver, in Hertfordshire, and called it Verulamium.

Now, in Verulamium, there lived a man named Alban. Late one night, this man was coming home to his house in the city, when he thought he saw someone lurking in the shadows near his door.

"Hullo!" said he to himself. "Is this an enemy, or just a beggar?" Aloud, he said:

"Come along now, out of that. Quickly!"

Thereupon, there stepped from out of the shadows a little old man, a most harmless and friendly-looking person. He was wearing the dress of a Christian priest.

Alban laughed.

"Was it only you?" he said. "I thought it was a beggar at least. Whatever made you hide there like that?"

"Why, to tell you the truth," explained the priest, "I thought you were a Roman soldier."

"And pray," said Alban, still rather amused, "what have you done, that you should hide from the soldiers? You look harmless enough."

"Oh! but I'm not," said the priest, his eyes twinkling. "You might not think it, but I'm an Enemy of Society, a Menace to the State, and a Dangerous Criminal. At least, so they tell me."

Alban's smile had given place to a frown.

" What *is* all this ? " he demanded.

The little priest was serious too, now. " It is quite simple," said he. " I am a Christian."

" But there are many Christians in the city ! " exclaimed Alban. " I'm not one myself, but they always seem to me to be quite well behaved, decent sort of people."

" The Emperor does not think so," answered the priest. " Perhaps you have not heard of his new Decree ? "

The Emperor he meant was Diocletian, Emperor of Rome. At that time, Britain was part of the Roman Empire, so that what the Emperor commanded in Rome was carried out in Britain. And the Emperor had commanded the persecution of the Christians.

" New Decree ? " repeated Alban. " Yes, now you mention it, I did hear of one. Something about the Christians, wasn't it ? I'm afraid I didn't take very much notice."

" I expect it didn't seem very important to you," said the priest, gently. " To us, it was rather. You see, the Emperor has commanded that Christianity is to be stamped out all through his Empire. Anyone who says he is a Christian will be arrested, and probably put to death. So you see "— and his eyes began to twinkle again— " according to the Emperor I am an extremely dangerous person, and it would be most unwise for you to be seen talking to me. I had better say good night," and he turned away.

But Alban said quickly :

" Where are you going ? Have you somewhere to sleep ? "

The priest hesitated.

" I thought of going into the woods," he said. " Some of our people have gone there already, I believe, and it is safer than——"

" Nonsense ! " cried Alban. " An old man like you needs a roof over his head at night. You had better come with me."

" Into your house ? " said the priest. " But that would be very dangerous—for you."

Alban shrugged his shoulders.

" That's all right," said he. " This way, and don't talk or you'll wake the household."

The priest hesitated a moment—then followed Alban into the house.

It was late. Even the servants were in bed. Alban led the priest to a tiny room. " You will be quite safe here," he said. " No one ever comes to this room. The bed is not too bad. I'll find you some supper."

And there the old priest lay hidden for some time. No one in the house even knew he was there except Alban himself and one very faithful servant, who brought his meals.

Alban took a great fancy to the old man, whose name was Amphibalus, and used often to slip along to his room to have a chat with him. Usually he found him saying his prayers or reading about Our Lord in the little book he carried. Always he was cheerful and contented : never worried or frightened, in spite of his great danger.

" There must be something in this Christianity," said Alban to himself. " I've a great mind to ask Amphibalus to explain it to me properly."

So he did, and the end of it was that Alban, too, became a Christian.

Now, beside having one very faithful servant, Alban had one very inquisitive one. A tall, clumsy fellow, with a great nose that seemed always snuffing around for trouble. He soon began to guess that there was some secret in the house. One day, hunting round to try to discover what it was, he found the very faithful servant alone in the kitchen, putting some dishes of food on a tray.

" What are you going to do with all that ? " he asked. " Has the Master got company ? "

" Mind your own business," replied the other, picking up the tray.

" Well, he can't be going to eat all that himself," persisted the inquisitive one.   " You can't tell *me*——"

" I'm not going to," replied the very faithful servant, and carried the tray off, leaving the inquisitive one simply dying of curiosity.

After that he absolutely had to try and try until he found out the secret.

" Queer things going on in our house," he told a friend of his, in the market one morning.   " Ah ! mighty queer things."

" Really ? " said his friend, " what sort of things ? Plots, and so on ? "

" Plots ! " snorted the inquisitive one contemptuously. " Plots are nothing to this !   It's my belief—" he lowered his voice mysteriously—" it's my belief the Master is *hiding a Christian !* "

" Whew ! " whistled the other.   " I wouldn't be in his shoes if that's it.   The Governor is down on these Christians like a ton of bricks."

Well, you know how it is when people start gossiping. In less than no time it had come to the ears of the Roman Governor that Alban was sheltering a Christian priest.

Next morning, just as he was getting up, Alban heard the steady tramp, tramp, that could only mean Roman soldiers.   He looked out of his window.   Yes, there they were !   Suddenly he realised that they were coming to his house.   Even as he did so, they were at the gate.   He saw the very inquisitive servant rush to open it, nearly falling over himself in his hurry.   The Captain spoke to him. Alban caught the word " priest."

Instantly, he understood.   Somehow, the Governor had found out that the priest was hiding there and had sent to seize him.

Alban stood in the middle of his room, thinking hard. In a few moments he had made up his mind what to do. Quickly, he crept into the priest's room : the old man was sleeping soundly.   Alban snatched up his hooded cloak, and crept out again.

As he came out of the room he met the very faithful servant.

"Master," the servant cried, "I was looking for you. There are soldiers——"

"Yes, I know," interrupted Alban. "They want the priest, but they shall not take him. I will go down and speak to them in a moment. Meanwhile, you wake Amphibalus, and see him safely out of the town."

"But—but Master," protested the bewildered servant.

"It's all right," said Alban, smiling. "Good-bye—and God bless you."

Then, before his servant could say any more, he stepped into his own room and closed the door.

As soon as he was inside, Alban slipped the priest's cloak on, completely hiding his own clothes, and drew the hood well over his face. Then he opened the door and walked quietly downstairs.

He found the Roman soldiers in the hall, watched by a group of trembling servants. The inquisitive one was making himself very busy. Cringing round the soldiers one minute; the next, frightening his fellow-servants with tales of the awful things that would happen to them if the Christian priest were not given up at once.

Alban walked straight up to the Captain.

"I am ready to come with you," he said.

The Captain saw the priest's cloak—that was enough for him. "Good," said he. "The Governor wants a word with you! Tie him up, men. Ready? About turn—quick march!"

Alban was marched off to the Governor.

As it happened, the Governor was standing at his altar, offering sacrifices to his Roman gods, when the prisoner was brought before him.

"The Christian priest, Excellency," said the Captain, saluting.

"Good," said the Governor. He glanced carelessly at the quiet figure standing before him with bent head and hood so closely drawn that his face was almost hidden. Then he looked again, more keenly.

"Put back your hood," he said sharply.

Alban did so.

"Idiots !" burst out the Governor, turning upon the soldiers, "you have brought the wrong man !"

The Captain began to stammer some explanation.

"That will do," snapped the Governor. "You had better go back at once and see if you can get the right one."

The soldiers tramped out.

In a towering rage, the Governor turned upon Alban, and commanded him to sacrifice to the Roman gods then and there. But Alban would not. Again and again the Governor threatened and commanded. Alban stood firm.

"You are the most stubborn fellow I ever met !" cried the Governor at last. "What is your name ?"

"That," replied Alban calmly, "is no concern of yours. If you want to know my religion, I will tell you. I am a Christian."

"I asked your name !" thundered the Governor. "Tell it me instantly !"

"Very well," replied Alban. "I am called Alban. And," he added proudly, "I worship and adore the Living God who created all things."

"Much good may it do you !" scoffed the Governor. "If you want to enjoy eternal life, you had better sacrifice to our gods at once."

"Gods !" cried Alban, "they are not gods, but devils."

And nothing would make him offer sacrifice on the Roman altar.

Then the Governor became really furious, and ordered him to be whipped, but still Alban would not give in. At last, when the Governor saw that there was nothing to be done with him, he ordered him to be put to death.

Surrounded by soldiers, with the Executioner walking before him, Alban was led out to execution. They marched through the town towards the river, for it was on a hill on the further side that the execution was to take place.

When they reached the bridge over the Ver they found a huge crowd waiting, for Alban was rather an important person in Verulamium.   The soldiers halted.

" H'm," murmured the Captain.   " Bit awkward."

Indeed, the crowd was so thick that it was impossible to get to the bridge.

" What are we stopping for ? " asked Alban.

" Crowd," answered the Captain.   " But don't imagine you've any chance of rescue.   Anyone who tries that is going to be unlucky."

" I don't imagine anything of the kind," answered Alban calmly, " but I should like to get on and—well—get it over."

Well, Alban and his captors at last managed to cross the river, either by a ford, or because, as one legend says, the river parted to let them pass.   The hillside was beautiful with grass and flowers. Slowly, they climbed to the chosen spot, followed by a great crowd of people, some sympathetic, some just curious.

At last they stopped.   They had reached the place of execution.

" Stand back there !   Stand back there ! " shouted the soldiers, pushing at the crowd with the butts of their spears.

" All ready, Executioner ? " cried the Captain.

The Executioner came slowly forward. He looked pale, and he was trembling so much that he could hardly hold his great sword.

" Get on—get on—" urged the Captain impatiently. " What's the matter with you ? "

Slowly, the Executioner raised his sword—held it a moment above his head—then flung it away !

A gasp went through the crowd.

" I can't !   I won't ! " shouted the Executioner.   " *I'm a Christian too !*   And now," he added defiantly, " **you** can do what you like about it."

Alban went to him, and took his hand.

Unfortunately, this unexpected happening made no difference to Alban, for another man was found then and there to do the Executioner's work.   It made a great deal of difference to the first Executioner though, for he was beheaded too.

Time passed.   The Romans went away, and were forgotten : their proud city of Verulamium fell into ruins. But Alban was not forgotten, and from those very ruins, long afterwards, a Cathedral was built in his honour, which stands to this day.

There is still a town there, too, on the River Ver, but its name has been changed.   It is called—but perhaps you can guess ?—St. Albans.

III

SAINT ETHELBERT OF KENT—
A CIVILISED KING

WHAT a lot of Saints there are named " Ethel " something ! St. Ethelwald, St. Ethelnoth, St. Etheldreda, two St. Ethelwolds, two St. Ethelberts, and *three* St. Ethelburgas !

The one in this story is Saint Ethelbert of Kent : he is my favourite because I think he was such a *civilised* kind of person.   I'll tell you why I think so at the end of the story : meantime you can be deciding what you think about it.

Saint Ethelbert began (in the year 560) by being King Ethelbert of Kent.   Those were the days when almost every county had its own king, but Ethelbert was so much more powerful than the others that he was sometimes called the King of the English.

Now, King Ethelbert and his subjects were pagans, but the King had married a Christian princess—Bertha, granddaughter of the King of France.   You might think that, when she married him, the King would try to make her change to his religion.   But no—far from that, he made it as easy as he could for her to go on being a Christian. She brought with her from France a Bishop, named Luihard, and the King allowed him to use a little church called St. Martin's, which had been built near the walls of Canterbury in the time of the Romans.   There, the Bishop held services, so that Queen Bertha, and perhaps some of her ladies who came from France with her, were able to

The King was baptised on Whit Sunday.

go to church, just as they had done at home, in spite of living in a pagan country.

So they went on for some time, the Queen worshipping God and the King worshipping Thor and Woden ; not quarrelling about it, but doing what is called "agreeing to differ."

Then, something important began to happen.

One day, as the King sat in his palace at Canterbury (Canterbury was the capital of the Kingdom of Kent), a page came to him. He could hardly speak for astonishment.

" P-please, Your M-majesty," he stammered, " there's a p-per—there's a p-per——"

" There's a what ? " said the King. " Speak up, boy."

The page swallowed, made a great effort, and said :

" Please, Your Majesty, there's a person to see you."

" Indeed ? " the King answered. " Well, that is not altogether unusual. Who is he, and what does he want ? "

" I—I—" began the page, getting all hot and bothered again, " I—I couldn't quite—I didn't exactly—" then, with a rush : " *He's a foreigner !* "

" Is that all ? " laughed the King. " Well, you know, there *are* other people in the world beside Angles and Saxons. Bring him to me. And for goodness sake," he added, " don't look at him like that. He won't bite ! "

The boy ran out, and presently ushered the stranger into the King's presence. The King looked eagerly to see who it was who had caused his page so much surprise.

It was a monk from Rome.

No wonder the boy was surprised ! Probably hardly anyone in Kent had ever seen a monk—let alone a foreign one—at that time. There had been monks, and priests too, in Britain before this, because Christianity came to Britain in the days of the Romans. But when the Angles and Saxons invaded Britain, and settled there, they drove the Britons into the mountains and moors of Wales and Cornwall, and Christianity with them, while they, the invaders, set up their own old pagan gods in England.

Then the Christian churches fell into ruins, and the Christian faith was forgotten, and nobody knew or cared about either of them.

However, the King did not find the visitor quite so strange as his page had done because of Bishop Luihard. In any case, he was much too polite to show any surprise, but said graciously :

" Greeting, stranger.   What can I do for you ? "

" Your Majesty," replied the monk, " I bring a message from Father Augustine, who has been sent by His Holiness Pope Gregory to preach to the people of this island the gospel of Christianity and to tell them the story of Our Lord Jesus Christ."

The King looked thoughtful.

" Where is this—Father Augustine ? " he asked.

" In the Isle of Thanet," the monk answered.   " A party of us have just landed there and we want to ask your permission to preach to your people."

Again the King considered.

At last he said :

" Of course I have *heard* of this faith of yours.   In fact, as perhaps you know, the Queen herself is a Christian. But then, she was one when she married me.   Her people are Christians.   But as to preaching your faith throughout my Kingdom, and turning us all into Christians—that is another matter."

" Then what," asked the monk, " shall I tell Father Augustine ? "

" Ask him to stay where he is for a few days," replied the King, " while I think the matter over, and I will give orders that your party is to be fed and looked after properly while you are waiting."

The monk thanked him and went back to tell Augustine what the King had said.

" This," said King Ethelbert to himself, when he was alone, " is something really important.   I think I'll go and have a word with Bertha about it."

He rose and went to the Queen's apartments.

"My dear," said he, "I've had a rather interesting visitor. A Christian monk from Rome. It seems that a party of them have landed in Thanet and want to preach to us. Augustine, I think he said, was the name of their leader."

The Queen was quite excited.

"Do let them come, Ethelbert," she begged. "It would be wonderful if Kent could be a Christian Kingdom. I've always hoped," she went on eagerly, "that you would be a Christian some day. And now, it really seems as if——"

"Gently, gently, my dear," said Ethelbert. "Don't let us go too fast. Remember, this is all very strange to me. I must think it over carefully."

Well, the King did think it over, and at last he decided to go himself to the Isle of Thanet and hear what Augustine had to say.

"The fairest thing is to let him tell me exactly what Christianity is," he said to himself. "Until I know that, I cannot judge what to do. I suppose," he added thoughtfully, "I might have asked Bertha all about it long ago—but I just didn't think of it."

So King Ethelbert went to Thanet with his attendants. He must have had a very queer idea of Christians, for he arranged to meet Augustine in the open air, lest he should cast a spell over him. Spells and charms were supposed to be harmless in the open.

Some seats were therefore arranged under an oak tree, and there the King sat, surrounded by his attendants, to await the coming of Augustine and his monks.

Presently, they heard music, and looking in the direction from which it came they saw a procession moving towards them.

First came Augustine. He was a head and shoulders taller than the rest, and very noble looking. After him streamed a long file of about forty monks, carrying a silver cross and a picture of Our Lord, and singing as they came.

The King received them graciously, and made Augustine sit down before him.

" Now," said he, " tell me—what *is* this Christianity ? "

Then Augustine began to speak.

At first, only the King listened properly. The rest of his Court fidgeted, or stood with downcast eyes, looking bored, or gazed at Augustine with a superior smile. But, gradually, as the story of Our Lord unfolded, the fidgety ones stopped fidgeting, the bored ones looked up, and looked interested, and the superior ones forgot to look superior. Except for the voice of Augustine, there was not a sound. Even the birds were silent, as though they, too, were listening.

At last he ceased speaking. For a few moments there was a rather thrilling silence. Then the King spoke.

" What you tell us," said he, " is most beautiful. What you promise, most wonderful. But it is all very new and strange to me. I can't believe all that you say at once and give up everything that I and my people have held sacred for so long. However, since you have come so far to tell us all this (and I can see you believe it is true, and better than anything we tell of our gods), we will not hurt you, but treat you as our guests. I will see that you have food and drink and everything you need while you are here, and you can preach as much as you like. If you can convert any of my people, you may."

So it was arranged. The King gave Augustine and his monks a house in Canterbury to live in, and they were allowed to use the Church of St. Martin, where Bishop Luihard held services for Queen Bertha. The King let them preach quite openly to his people, as he had said, and the people liked what they heard so much, and were so struck by the good and simple lives of Augustine and his monks, that very soon some of them decided to be Christians.

Queen Bertha was ever so pleased about this, but when the King himself decided to become a Christian, too, she was simply delighted.

"You can't be more delighted than I am," the King told her. He was so pleased that he gave up his royal palace in Canterbury for Augustine to live in.

The King was baptised on Whit Sunday in the year 597. It was a very important thing for England, because, though he had said to Augustine, "You may convert whom you can," naturally it was much easier to do this when so great and powerful a King was himself a Christian.

For one thing, the King did all he could to help, and was as eager as Augustine to make new Christians.

"The only thing is," warned Augustine, "you mustn't try to force anyone. The whole point is for them to decide to be Christians because they want to, and because they feel sure that Christianity is true."

"Of course," agreed Ethelbert. "You *can't* make anyone believe anything, however true it is. I might make them all pretend to be Christians for fear of what I would do to them if they weren't, but that wouldn't be the same thing at all, and even if I didn't know the difference, God certainly would."

Augustine smiled.

"I see you have the right idea," said he.

So the King set to work to try to *persuade* people to be Christians, and succeeded quite well. After a time he actually converted two other kings—Sebert, King of the East Saxons, and Redwald, King of the East Angles, though Redwald went back to Thor and Woden afterwards. But that was not Ethelbert's fault.

As for his own people, there were a good many pagans left among them, but, though the King could not help liking the Christians best, he always treated everyone alike, giving the same justice to both Christian and pagan.

And while he was helping to make new Christians, the King was also doing all he could to make sure that there should be plenty of churches for them. He gave Augustine and his monks permission to build new churches, and repair the old ones which had been built before the Angles and Saxons came : he founded St. Andrew's in Rochester,

c

St. Paul's in London, and the Church of SS. Peter and Paul outside the walls of Canterbury.   Last, but not least, inside the city he founded Christ Church—that is, Canterbury Cathedral, with Augustine as Archbishop.

And now for why I think he was so *civilised*.

Well, first, he was not afraid of new ideas—see how he received Augustine.   Next, he understood that conscience must be free—see how he refused to *force* anyone to be a Christian.   Lastly, he knew that justice must be the same for all.   And that's why I call him a truly civilised person. I hope you agree.

IV

SAINT HILDA—" MOTHER " OF NORTHUMBRIA

Bregusuid's Dream

WHEN people are worried they often dream a lot. That was how Bregusuid, Saint Hilda's mother, came to dream about her. Not that she was worried about Hilda, because she was not even born, but she *was* worried about her husband, Prince Hereric.

They were living in exile at the time—banished from their home by King Ethelfrid of Northumbria, and Bregusuid was always expecting something worse to happen. So that was why she worried, and this was what she dreamed :

She thought her husband had disappeared, and she was wandering about looking for him. She went on and on, seeking him, but she could not find him anywhere. At last, hot and tired, she threw off her cloak. Then she discovered that she was wearing a most marvellous necklace. She was not a bit surprised (you know how you take the most curious things for granted in dreams), but began to admire the necklace, forgetting all about poor Prince Hereric. As she looked at them, the jewels in the necklace began to glow like lamps, brighter and brighter, until their light filled the whole country. Then, as usually happens when things are getting really interesting, she woke up.

Her husband was sound asleep beside her.

" Hereric," she said, giving him a little shake, " I've had such a marvellous dream."

Caedmon stood up and sang before them.

" Eh ? " murmured the Prince, sleepily. " Have you, dear ? How—how marvellous. If I were you I'd go to sleep again. You might have another."

" You couldn't have two dreams like mine," replied Bregusuid, now wide awake. " Do listen."

" Yes, dear, I'm listening," replied the Prince, kindly, but not very enthusiastically, because like most people, though he loved to tell his own dreams, he really did not care much for hearing other people's.

However, Bregusuid was too excited to notice, but just went on telling her dream. " Don't you think it was marvellous ? " she concluded.

" Well," said her husband, doubtfully, " after all, any-one could dream about a necklace."

" Not with jewels that lit up the whole country," argued Bregusuid. " Besides, it wasn't a necklace really. I mean, it stood for something else. I'm sure it means that we are going to have a child who will be so good and so clever that she will be like a light shining all over the kingdom. Don't you agree with me, darling ? "

But Hereric was fast asleep.

Soon after that, about the year 614, Bregusuid did have a baby : a little girl, whom they named Hilda.

" What did I tell you ? " she exclaimed to her husband, triumphantly. " You remember my dream about the necklace ? That necklace stood for baby. She is going to be great some day ! "

Prince Hereric looked thoughtfully at his baby daughter.

" It's too soon to tell," he said cautiously.

Poor Hilda did not have a very good start in life, for while she was still quite little she was left an orphan. First her father was 'poisoned : then her mother died suddenly. Except for an elder sister, named Heresuid, Hilda was quite alone.

By this time King Ethelfrid was dead, and a new King had come to the throne. This was King Edwin, uncle of Prince Hereric. Like Hilda's parents he had been living in exile, constantly hunted from place to place by King Ethelfrid, and when at last his enemy was dead and he was able to return to his own home, he took with him his little grandniece, Hilda.

Presently the King married Princess Ethelberg of Kent, and Hilda, who lived at the Court, became fast friends with her.

Now, the new Queen was a Christian, but King Edwin and his people were still pagans. However, the King promised faithfully not to prevent Queen Ethelberg from going on being a Christian, and to make sure of this she brought with her from Kent the Bishop Paulinus. The Bishop was very pleased to go, for beside helping the Queen and her Christian attendants to keep true to their own faith, he meant to try to persuade the King and his people to be Christians too.

King Edwin was quite willing. " Certainly," said he. " You tell the people about your God as much as you like —I don't mind. If any of them want to be Christians, I shan't stop them."

So Paulinus preached and the people listened. Unfortunately, they still went on worshipping Thor and Odin and all their old pagan gods. It was very disheartening.

" I don't believe they really listen properly," said the Queen, who, being a Christian herself, naturally took a great interest in the matter.

But there was one person who did listen properly. That was Hilda. She was now a rather serious little girl of about twelve, and Paulinus had already noticed her. It seemed to him that whenever he preached, there she was, as near to him as she could get, her great, solemn eyes fixed on his face, simply drinking in his words. At last he asked the King who she was.

" So that is the younger daughter of Prince Hereric ! " he exclaimed, when he had heard her story. " What a clever, interesting face ! She will make a very fine woman one day."

" She's a dear," said the Queen. " She and I are the best of friends. I wish she were a Christian, though."

" She will be soon," replied the Bishop confidently.

He was right, though it came about in a different way from what he and the Queen expected.

For nearly a year Paulinus had been preaching to the Northumbrians, and the Northumbrians had listened politely and gone on worshipping Thor and Odin, when one day, something happened which changed everything.

Someone tried to murder the King.

It was on Easter Eve that a messenger came to Court asking to see King Edwin. He had, he said, a message from the King of the West Saxons, but what he really had was a poisoned dagger. The message gave him an excuse to get near the King. The moment he did so he whipped out his dagger, and struck ! Luckily for the King, one of his thanes threw himself in the way, but the murderer struck so hard, that the dagger went right through him to the King.

There was wild confusion in the Court. Some seized the messenger, some ran to the King, some clustered round the dying thane. Then, in the midst of it all, one of the Queen's ladies came to tell the King that the Queen had just had a baby girl !

The King sat down and mopped his brow (he was not much hurt—the poison had all been used up on the poor thane).

" Well ! " said he, " this *has* been a day ! I've only just escaped being murdered, and now I've got a little daughter ! I think we ought all to go and praise the gods."

He meant Thor and Odin and all the pagan gods, of course. But before anyone could agree, Paulinus spoke :

" You should thank God and Our Lord Jesus Christ, Your Majesty," said he. " For a long while I have been praying that He would bless and protect you and your Queen, and now you see that He has."

" Did *your* God do it ? " said King Edwin. " Are you *sure* ? Then I'll tell you what I'll do. If He will give me long life, and victory over my enemy, I will give up all the other gods and serve Him only. And not only that," he added, " I will give my new baby girl to belong to Him and serve Him for ever."

Well, the King did defeat his enemy, and remembering his promise he allowed his baby daughter to be christened by Bishop Paulinus.   With her were baptised twelve other members of the royal household, and one of these was Hilda.   She was about thirteen years old.

As for King Edwin, he did not actually become a Christian at once, but he asked Paulinus to teach him all about it, and about a year later he was baptised with all his Counsellors and many of his people.

By the time Hilda was grown up, Northumbria was a Christian country.   She was still living at Court, the friend of the Queen, and like an auntie to the little Princess, who was named Eanfled, and her brother Wuscfrea, who was born later.

There must have been many princes and nobles who would have liked to marry her, but Hilda had another idea. She wanted to be a nun.   Unfortunately, there were no convents in Northumbria.   It had not been Christian very long, you see.

" Well, it can't be helped," said Hilda to herself. " Perhaps there will be a chance later on.   Meanwhile I must just be as good as I can without being a nun."

And so she was.   In fact the old books say that she " lived nobly."

It was not until she was thirty-three that Hilda had a chance to carry out her plan.   You remember she had a sister ?   Well, this sister had married, and had one son, and then been left a widow, after which she went into a convent at Chelles, near Paris.

" That's an idea ! " thought Hilda.   " I'll go to Chelles, too.   It would be nice for Heresuid and I to be together."

The Dream's Fulfilment

Travelling was not then the simple thing that it is now. You could not just say, " I'll catch the ten o'clock boat train." You had to wait for a ship—sometimes quite a long time.

Knowing this, Hilda decided to go first to East Anglia, where her nephew, Heresuid's son, was King, and to stay with him while waiting for a ship. Had she got one quickly, it might have made a lot of difference to her, and to England, but she had to wait some months.

While she was waiting to go *from* Britain, there travelled *to* Britain Bishop Aidan of Lindisfarne. He had been abroad and was now returning to the great Monastery of Lindisfarne, off the Northumbrian coast, which he had founded. When he heard that Hilda was thinking of going to Chelles, he exclaimed :

" But why need she go abroad ? She is just the kind of person we want here ! I must go and have a chat with her about this."

" My daughter," said he, when they had exchanged greetings, " what is this I hear about your going to Chelles ? "

" It's quite true, Father," replied Hilda. " I'm only waiting for a ship. I've always wanted to be a nun, and as Heresuid is at Chelles, I thought——"

" Wait a moment, my dear," interrupted Aidan. " I quite understand your wanting to be with your sister, but we cannot spare you. Britain needs women like you. Won't you stay and serve God in your own country ? "

" But there are no convents in Northumbria," objected Hilda.

" Then why not start one ? " Aidan suggested. " I will give you a little piece of land on which to build a house, and perhaps you can get a few women like yourself to join you. Then you can start a convent of your own. What do you say ? "

Hilda was delighted at the idea. " I believe I could do it," she said. " I should love to try."

" And so you shall," said Bishop Aidan.

The land he gave her was on the banks of the River Wear. There she settled down with a few companions. For a year they lived there, and Bishop Aidan, who was watching, and helping when necessary, was so pleased with the way Hilda managed everything, that he presently chose her to be the Abbess of a much larger monastery which had been started at Hartlepool, in place of the Abbess Heiu, who had retired. This, of course, was much harder, but Hilda was such a splendid organiser, that she soon had everything running beautifully.

For some years she was Abbess at Hartlepool. Then came her third and last change. This time she went to a new monastery at a place named Streaneshalch. (We call it Whitby now, which is much easier.) It was here, at Whitby, that her best and greatest work was done.

It was what is called a double monastery—that is to say, there was one great house for monks, and another for nuns, and over all ruled the Abbess Hilda, so wisely, kindly and well that she was soon famous all over her country. Everyone loved her and looked up to her. Kings and princes asked her advice on all their difficulties—and took it, too ; the great Bishop Aidan himself came to consult with her, and far beyond the borders of Northumbria the people thought and spoke of her as " Mother."

The rules at Whitby were strict, but just. Nobody kept anything for themselves alone but all shared everything in common, and everyone, high or low, was treated exactly the same. You can judge how good it was by the fact that no fewer than five Bishops came from among the monks of Whitby.

But it was not Kings and Bishops alone whom Hilda helped and encouraged. She was just as ready to do everything she could for the poor and simple people. There was one in particular—Caedmon. I expect you have heard of him.

Caedmon was a cowherd on the monastery lands ; a simple soul and rather shy. He was happy enough in his own quiet way, but he had one great trouble, one of those troubles that seem just silly to other people, but can make the person who has it feel dreadfully unhappy. It was just this—he could not sing.

Quite a lot of people cannot sing, but no one would be likely to bother much about the matter nowadays. In Caedmon's time, however, things were different. Practically everybody could sing and play the harp a little. They had to do something in the long dark evenings, with no wireless or pictures, and no books to read. So they used to gather in each other's houses and sit round the fire singing and playing, sometimes in turn, sometimes together. They would go on all the evening, passing the harp from hand to hand and having a delightful time. So you see, it was important to be able to sing, and play the harp a little. But Caedmon could do neither, and when those evenings began he used to feel perfectly awful. He would sit there, watching the harp passing round the circle, and the nearer it got to him the worse he felt, until when it reached, say, the next person but one to himself, he would rise, mutter something about " have to be going " and slip away home.

The others would look at each other and smile, and say, " Poor old Caedmon, " but soon they would be rolling out another song and Caedmon would be quite forgotten.

Now, one evening Caedmon and some others were up at a friend's house, having such a jolly time, when out came that wretched harp again !   The others set up a cheer, but poor old Caedmon's heart sank.   Then someone struck up a song, benches were drawn into a circle round the fire, the host threw on a fresh log, and the whole party prepared for a thoroughly good time.   All but Caedmon. He sat as near to the door as possible, feeling wretched.

Nearer came the harp, nearer and nearer.

" You ought to have a go," whispered the man next to him.   " Go on ! it's ever so easy ! "

Caedmon shook his head, wishing he could sink through the floor.   One singer had finished.   " Bravo ! " cried the others (except the next man, who was too busy struggling to remember the words of his own song).   Now the harp was only three places away !   Caedmon watched it as if it had been a wild beast stalking him.   At last he could bear it no longer.

" I—I think I'll go and have a look at the horses," he muttered, and crept out.   As he closed the door behind him he heard someone say, " Poor old Caedmon."

He was to sleep in the stable that night, for it was his turn to look after the horses.   Well—at least they could not sing or play the harp !

" I'm better here, with the beasts," he sighed, as he lay down in the straw beside them.   " The dumb beasts."

One of the mares opened her great soft eyes and nuzzled him gently.   He stroked her velvety nose.

" A great, stupid fellow I am," he told her, " but you don't mind, do you, lass, if stupid old Caedmon can't sing ? "   He sighed again, pulled some straw over himself, and fell asleep.

That night he had a dream that changed his whole life.

He dreamed that a stranger came to him, there in the stable, and said :

" Caedmon, sing to me."

" I can't sing," answered Caedmon.   " Not a note, I

can't. That's why I came out here, with the dumb beasts."

"All the same," said the stranger, "you shall sing to me."

Caedmon's heart began to beat fast. For the first time in his life he had a feeling—"*perhaps I could sing after all.*"

"What shall I sing?" he whispered.

And the stranger answered calmly:

"Sing the 'Creation of the World.'"

Not some simple little song about nothing in particular. Not a hymn or folk song that everyone knew, but the Creation of the World! Just that!

And Caedmon, who had never in his life before sung a note or made a verse, found himself singing a marvellous poem all about God and how He created the world. On and on he sang, never pausing, never in the least doubt as to the next word. Forgetting that he could not sing—he just sang.

And then he woke up.

People often have dreams in which they find themselves being wonderfully clever and doing something which they could never do while they were awake, but when they do wake they find that they are no cleverer than usual. The marvellous part about Caedmon's dream was that when he woke he could remember the whole of the poem he had made. What was more—*he was able to make up some more verses.*

"There's something strange about this," said Caedmon to himself, sitting up in the straw and gazing about the stable as though he had never seen it before in his life. "I'd better go and see Steward about it."

"Well, Caedmon," said the Steward when the old man presented himself, "what is it?"

"Well, Sir," replied Caedmon gravely, "I—I'm afraid I've turned into a—a sort of poet. In the night, like."

"Dear me," said the Steward, trying not to smile, "what makes you think that?"

" Because I've made a poem, Sir," confessed Caedmon. " At least, I—I *think* it's a poem.   It was this way, Sir——" and he told the story of his dream.

" This is important," said the Steward, now quite serious.   " Come, we will go and see the Abbess Hilda about it."

So they came to Hilda and again Caedmon told his story.   She was even more interested than the Steward. " Can you remember the verses ? " she asked.

" Yes, Mother," answered Caedmon.   " I never set out to do it," he added earnestly.   " Something came over me——"

Hilda smiled.   " Perhaps God inspired you," she said, " as He does all true poets.   But I won't try to judge for myself.   We will see what others think."

She called a committee of the cleverest monks at Whitby to hear Caedmon's poem, and Caedmon, much astonished at himself, stood up and sung it before them.

" But this is wonderful ! " they cried.   " And you composed it yourself ? "

" Yes, Reverend Fathers," admitted Caedmon, adding hastily, " In a dream, do you see."

The committee talked it over with Hilda.   Was this just an accident, or had Caedmon a real gift for poetry ? They decided to give him a test.   They chose a piece out of the Bible and told him to try and turn it into verse as he had done the story of the creation.   Caedmon went away.   Next day he was back with a new poem as good as the first.

" This is poetry indeed ! " said Hilda, and all the monks in the committee agreed.   " Caedmon is a true poet," she said.   " We must see that his gift is not wasted."

She would not let him go on being a cowherd any longer.   He must join the monastery, she said, and be a monk, so that he could spend his whole time in using this great new power. Caedmon wanted nothing better. From that time he spent his days in studying the scriptures and turning them into verse.   The man who could not so much as sing a rhyme to his friends round the fire was the first to write hymns in the English tongue. But for Hilda it might never have happened. If she had not recognised a poet when she found one, his first poem might also have been his last, and England might have waited much longer for her first poet.

Now all this time many changes had been happening in the world outside the monastery, in some of which Hilda herself had had a part. For one thing, King Edwin had died, and a new King named Oswy had come to the throne. Like Edwin he had a baby daughter, and like him he promised that if God would give him victory over his greatest enemy, his little girl should be dedicated to God's service. He won his victory, and the baby Elfleda was brought to Whitby to be brought up by Hilda and become a nun, and so well did Hilda teach and Elfleda learn, that when Hilda herself died Elfleda was made Abbess of Whitby in her place.

Hilda was sixty-six when she died. For the last seven years of her life she suffered from fever. She never gave in, however, but worked and taught just the same right to the end of her life.

The whole country grieved to hear of her illness, but the saddest of all was a nun named Begu, who lived at Hackness, a convent about thirteen miles from Whitby, and who loved Hilda most dearly.

One night, when Hilda had been ill about seven years, Begu woke suddenly. She thought she heard the sound of a passing bell, such as is rung when someone has just died. As she lay listening, it seemed to her as if there was no longer a roof above her, but she looked straight up to the sky, and the sky was lit with dazzling light.

She jumped up, and ran to the Head of the Convent.

" Reverend Mother," she cried, " I am sure our beloved Mother Hilda is dead. I have had a vision——"

Begu was so certain about it that the Mother Superior called all her nuns to church to pray for Hilda. All night they knelt there, and by morning they knew that Begu was

right, for with the dawn came messengers from Whitby—
the Abbess Hilda was dead.

I think she really was rather like a necklace. Her life
was the thread, and all the good things she did were the
jewels—jewels that filled the whole country with their light
while she lived, and even now are still part of our English
treasure.

V

SAINT MILDRED—A MERCIFUL
LADY

A Cruel Deed

HERE was once a king who had three daughters. His name was Merwald, and he was the son of King Penda of Mercia. Mercia was such a large kingdom that it was very difficult for one person to look after it properly. So King Penda said to his son : " You can be king of the southern part and rule it for me."

Then Merwald rode south, as his father had commanded : and he chose for his capital the town of Wenlock (which we call *Much* Wenlock), and he chose for his Queen a Kentish Princess named Ermenburga.

But what about the three fair daughters ? Well, they were called Milburga, Mildred and Mildgytha. (There was a son, too, but he died young, so he does not come into this story.)

The royal family at Wenlock were a very happy family. Queen Ermenburga had to do most of the bringing up, because the King so often had to ride off to war, but she did it very well and, as she and the King were both Christians, there was no argument about that, anyhow. Whenever the King could spare the time he would hurry home, and then they would all sit round the fire and talk about " what the girls are going to do when they grow up."

" I should like to be a nun," announced Milburga, the eldest, one day.

The people brought her food and asked her to pray for them.

" Then," said the Queen, smiling at her, " you will have to work very hard to learn how. I think you had better go to Leominster as soon as possible and begin."

The King agreed. In fact, he got quite enthusiastic about it. It was he who had built the monastery at Leominster.

" Listen," said he, " I'll tell you what I'll do. While Milburga is at Leominster, I'll build an Abbey here at Wenlock. Then, when she is old enough, and good enough, she can come and be the Abbess."

Milburga looked very pleased.

" *I* should like to be a nun too," said Mildgytha, who was the baby of the family.

" You two little ones can both come to my abbey if you like," said Milburga, in a rather elder-sisterly tone.

" I haven't said I'm going to be a nun yet," remarked Mildred, the middle one.

" Well, aren't you ? " exclaimed Mildgytha, astonished.

Mildred considered. " I don't know," she said. " I think I'll wait and see what my Guardian Angel says about it."

" How do you know you've got one ? " demanded Milburga.

Mildred opened a pair of very blue eyes very wide.

" *Of course* I've got a Guardian Angel," she said. " I've often seen him."

" Yes, but——" began her sisters together, but the Queen put in gently :

" Now girls, no arguments. Mildred will know what to do when the time comes."

When she and the King were alone, she said :

" I shall keep the two younger ones with me for a little while longer. There is plenty of time. I don't want them to be nuns just because Milburga is, but only if they feel they really must."

" That's true," agreed the King. " As you say, there is no hurry for them."

I may as well tell you before we go any further, that

Milburga did become Abbess of Wenlock, and Mildgytha was a nun too, and they are both saints. But this story is about Mildred.

Before Mildred had time to decide what she was going to do when she grew up, something happened which decided it for her.

One morning, one of the Queen's ladies came smiling to her, crying :

" Messengers from Kent, Madam ! Messengers from Kent ! "

The Queen jumped up eagerly.

" Bring them ! Bring them ! " she cried.

She was always delighted to have news from Kent, for though her parents were dead, she had two young brothers who lived there, and King Egbert of Kent was her cousin and her brothers' guardian, so she still thought of Kent as home.

But this time, as soon as she saw the messengers' faces, she wished they had not come. She could tell that they brought bad news.

They knelt before her, and offered her a letter.

" What is it ? " she said, half afraid to take it. " What has happened ? Tell me !"

The messengers were silent a moment. At last one spoke.

" Your brothers are dead, Madam," he said.

" My brothers dead ! " exclaimed the Queen. She had not seen them since they were little, but she had often heard what charming boys they were. And now they were dead !

" But how did it happen ? " she asked. " Please tell me everything ! "

Again the messenger hesitated. Then, sadly and reluctantly, he told this story :

King Egbert had always treated the two young princes kindly, but there was one at the Court who seemed to be against them from the first. This was one of the King's men, named Thunor. He had made up his mind that the princes were dangerous, and was forever hinting to King Egbert that they would try to take his throne.

"They'd be best out of the way, Your Majesty," he said one day for the hundredth time. "Or one of these days you'll wake up and find they've helped themselves to your throne."

"What," cried the King. "Those nice lads? I'm sure they've never thought of such a thing."

"Don't you believe it, Sire," growled Thunor. "I'll be bound they're plotting against you. Or if they haven't started yet, they soon will. Now look here, Sire, what about putting them quietly out of the way? I could arrange it as easily as—as——"

"That will do!" said the King. "I don't want to hear another word."

But Thunor would not let him alone. He kept hinting and hinting, until the King began to wonder whether he was right, and the princes were traitors.

Then, one morning, as the King was getting ready to go hunting, Thunor sidled up to him and whispered:

"There'll be a good chance to get rid of those princes to-day—while everyone is out hunting. I could arrange it easily—easily. What do you say, Your Majesty? Shall I——"

The King opened his lips to say "No," but somehow he didn't. Instead, he just turned away, pretending not to hear.

But all the time he was hunting he felt terribly uncomfortable, and didn't enjoy himself a bit. "I wish I had forbidden Thunor——" he thought. Then he laughed at himself. "Ridiculous! Of course he wouldn't dare!"

All the same, he felt half afraid to go home at the end of the day's sport. The moment they came in sight of the palace gates he saw that something was different. He checked his horse, and pointed.

"What's *that*?" he said.

From the roof a queer beam of light seemed to slant upwards to the sky. "What's that?" the King repeated.

Then, before anyone could answer him, he leapt from his horse and dashed indoors, shouting : " Thunor—send me Thunor at once ! "

" The princes—the princes," he thought, as he paced the great hall, waiting for Thunor. Why the strange beam of light should make him think of them he could not tell, but it *had*, and he was afraid.

Then Thunor stood before him. There was a self-satisfied smile on his cruel face.

" Where are the two princes ? " demanded the King.

" That's all right, my Lord King," replied Thunor, rubbing his hands and smiling horribly, " that's quite all right.   You've nothing to worry about——"

" *Where are the princes ?* " thundered the King. " Answer me ! "

Thunor bowed, cringingly. Then he beckoned the King towards the throne. " There ! " he whispered, pointing. " *Underneath.* No one will guess. Nothing to worry——"

Suddenly he looked up, and saw the King's face. The self-satisfied smile died away from his own, and an ugly look of fear came in its place. He licked his lips.

" I have only done what Your Majesty commanded," he muttered. " I—I was only carrying out your——"

" Dead ! " said the King. A moment he stood, looking straight at Thunor, yet not seeming to see him. At last he said :

" Yes, I am to blame. I should have forbidden it. I am the real murderer."

Then he turned and walked out of the hall.

Now, in those days, a man was not hanged for murder, but he had to pay a fine to the dead man's relatives, and beside that to do penance according to what the Church decided. Usually, he was exiled for seven years and sent to wander in strange lands, barefoot, like a beggar.

So King Egbert sent to the Archbishop of Canterbury, and the Archbishop came to see him, and the King told him what had happened.

"It was my fault," said he sadly. "I shall pay the fine, of course. But tell me what penance I must do as well."

The Archbishop looked at him long and gravely.

"Did you know what Thunor was going to do?" he asked.

"Not for certain," replied the King. "But I should have known, for I know Thunor. I'm quite willing to accept the blame."

"H'm," said the Archbishop, thoughtfully. "A king has great responsibilities, my son. And now, as to your penance. I shall give you none, but this I command you. Send for Queen Ermenburga, the sister of these boys, and let her choose what your penance shall be."

That was the bad news which brought the messengers from Kent to Wenlock.

The Queen was very much upset. She hardly remembered her brothers, it was so long since she had seen them, but it was a great shock to hear that they had been murdered. She set off at once for Canterbury, taking Mildred with her.

At Canterbury, King Egbert and the Archbishop were awaiting her in the King's Great Hall. It was a terribly solemn occasion. There was the Archbishop very grave, but kind, with his clerks: there was King Egbert, very pale and sad and dignified, with his nobles: there was Queen Ermenburga, very gentle, with her attendants, and there was Mildred, very solemn, and wondering whatever was going to happen.

The King greeted the Queen, and told her again the story of her murdered brothers. Then he said: "The fine is here, ready according to the law. And now, tell me, Madam, what else must I do for penance?"

When the King ceased speaking there was deep silence in the hall. Everyone was wondering what dreadful thing Queen Ermenburga would demand in return for her brothers' lives.

At last the Queen spoke. Her voice was gentle, yet so

clear that every word was heard even at the farthest end of the hall.

She said :

" There is no penance, my Lord King. I forgive you —just as I hope Our Lord will forgive me for all the wrong things I have done," and she smiled at him very sweetly.

A long sigh of relief ran round the hall. The King's men relaxed suddenly, and his youngest page whispered : " It's like ' forgive us our trespasses——' "

But the Queen had not finished. " We have no need to worry about my brothers," she went on, " they are quite safe now. It is you, Sire, I am thinking of, because you have murder, like a dark stain, on your soul. So listen : You shall give me land on which I will build an Abbey where the pure in heart shall pray for you until you too are pure again."

In a low voice, the King answered :

" Most gladly will I give you the land. How much shall it be, and where ? "

Ermenburga thought a minute. Then she said :

" The Abbey shall be in the Isle of Thanet. You shall give me as much land there as my tame deer can run over in a morning." And suddenly, she drew Mildred forward. " And in return," said she, " I will give you my daughter Mildred. She shall be the Abbess, and pray for you all her life."

Then the King fell on his knees, crying :

" Now I am sure I shall be forgiven ! "

As for Mildred, she was too surprised to say a word. She was thrilled with the idea, but a little frightened, too. However, she was very sorry for King Egbert, and only too pleased to help him, so she just smiled at him timidly, as much as to say, " I'll do the best I can."

So that was settled. The Archbishop gave everyone his blessing, and then the King, the Queen, Mildred, and all their attendants rode to the King's Court at Eastry.

The nobles riding behind the King were in good spirits.

"Well," said one, "We got out of that very well indeed—thanks to two most merciful ladies."

"Don't be too sure," growled Thunor, who was riding near him.

The other lifted his brows. "Hey! what have you to grumble about?" he cried. "Think yourself lucky the Queen did not ask for your head!"

But Thunor continued to mutter and scowl all the way to Eastry. "As much land as her deer can run over! That's a nice thing! Some woman's trick, I'll be bound."

It certainly was a rather peculiar idea, and everyone was anxious to see how it would work out. So it was a large and rather excited party which set out for Thanet. The only one who seemed quite unconcerned was the deer.

They had first to cross the River Wantsume (for in those days the Isle of Thanet really *was* an island). Then they rode right across to Westgate, which was to be the starting place.

The Queen was rather afraid that so many strangers might frighten the deer, so the King said that he and his men would keep at a little distance, from which they cou'd watch, without being in the way. This being agreed, the Queen called the deer to her, stroked its nose and sleek sides, kissed it between the ears, and sent it off. Away it went, while she and Mildred with their attendants, followed after. The deer was used to running just ahead of its mistress's horse, so it was not at all shy, but trotted happily along, enjoying itself very much, and quite unconscious of how important it was.

Meanwhile, the King and his people were watching anxiously to see how much of the Kingdom was to be given away. Or rather, the King's men watched anxiously. The King himself was still far too sorry about the poor little princes to care about land. Beside, he was not the kind of person to give something and then grudge it.

But Thunor was. Thunor was simply furious about the whole thing. Why he should care, if the King did not, I cannot imagine. Perhaps, in his own selfish way, he loved the King and did not like to see him lose anything. It seems strange that he should be there at all, instead of being banished or imprisoned or something, for after all he did kill the princes. However, his punishment was only just round the corner.

The King's party had halted, on a height overlooking the town of Minster. Suddenly, Thunor snatched at the King's arm, crying :

" Look ! Look ! See where that wretched little deer is going ! Right round Minster ! Do you mean to lose the town, Sire——"

The King said nothing, but drew his arm from under Thunor's hand. The nobles were all looking rather anxious. This really was rather too much of a good thing.

But Thunor simply could not bear it. With a shout, he galloped forward, meaning to head the deer off before it could reach the town. Unluckily for him, there lay, right across his path, a deep chalk pit. Before he knew what was happening, he fell crashing into it and was killed instantly.

Well, the deer ran fast and far, and scooped a great piece out of the Isle of Thanet, with the town of Minster somewhere about the middle. Then the Queen and King Egbert went down to see about choosing a site for the Abbey. They found a place near the town where there had once been a pagan temple, and decided to build it there, and to call it the Abbey of Minster-in-Thanet.

All the time they were discussing it, King Egbert was wondering about Mildred. " She is very young, and not even a nun yet," he thought. " She can't possibly be ready by the time the Abbey is." But he did not like to mention it. At last he said thoughtfully :

" The Abbey will take some time to build——"

" Yes," agreed the Queen, energetically, " but even so it will be finished long before Mildred has learned all she needs to know. It seems to me that I had better be Abbess myself until she is ready."

And so it was arranged. While the Abbey was being

built, the Queen went to a monastery at Lyminge to be trained as a nun, taking Mildgytha with her, because she, too, wanted to be a nun, if you remember. As for King Merwald—he had decided to give up being a king, and be a monk instead. So he went to the Abbey at Wenlock, where Milburga was Abbess. It was a double Abbey with one house for the monks and one for the nuns, and King Merwald became Prior of the monks' part, so it all fitted in beautifully.

From Novice to Abbess

AND Mildred? She went to Chelles, in France, where there was a rather special Abbey. It was quite exciting, going off on her own—or at least, without any of the family. The Abbess at Chelles was very pleased to have her and she soon settled down, determined to work hard, so as to be ready for being Abbess of Minster-in-Thanet later on. She learnt Latin and astronomy and embroidery, and all kinds of things, but what she liked best was learning how to copy and illuminate the sacred books. As soon as she could do it well enough, she began a Psalter. She copied every word herself and designed and painted all the illustrations.

"I shall give this to Mother when it is finished," she decided.

Then, just as she was getting along ever so well, there came a most unexpected and annoying interruption. A young man wanted to marry her !

First, he went to the Abbess of Chelles. She told him it was quite impossible, because Mildred was learning to be a nun, and as soon as she was old enough, and wise enough, and good enough, she would be an Abbess.

But the young man would not take no for an answer. "Do let me just ask her," he begged. "She's not even a nun yet, is she, so she can change her mind if she wants to." He begged so hard that at last the Abbess sent for Mildred and told her what he wanted.

But Mildred had no intention of changing her mind. First, because she didn't want to, secondly because though she was not yet a nun, she had promised God in her heart that she would be one, and thirdly because of having undertaken to pray for King Egbert.

So she said, "No, thank you," quite decidedly.

Then the young man grew terribly angry, and went away in a great rage, vowing that if she did not marry him of her own accord he would come and carry her off by force.

That frightened Mildred, for it seemed as if the Abbess was on the young man's side. She decided to run away. She would go home, she thought. She would be quite safe there.

Unknown to anyone, she slipped out of the Abbey and started to walk to the sea. It took a long time—whole days—and she was terribly tired when at last she reached the coast.

"Now," said she to herself, "I only want a ship."

She could not see any, so she walked along the shore until she came upon an old man mending some nets.

"Excuse me," said Mildred, "could you tell me how soon I could get a ship for the Isle of Thanet ? "

The old man shook his head.

"There'll be no more ships sailing until the spring," said he.

"No more ships!" cried Mildred. "Whatever's happened to them all?"

"Nothing has happened to *them*," answered the old man. "It's what has happened to the sea. The winter gales have begun, and not a ship can sail until they are over."

"Oh!" said Mildred, blankly. "Thank you."

Here was a nice state of affairs. No chance to get home until the spring. Whatever should she do?

"The one thing I must not do," said Mildred to herself, "is to get frightened. After all, I've got my Guardian Angel."

This thought so comforted her that she at once began to look for somewhere to live until the ships could sail. At last she found a place in some woods, where she managed to build herself a little hut or cell, and there she lived all the winter. It was very rough and hard, and she was ill part of the time, but she made the best of it, and even tried to hold little services by herself in her cell, and to help the peasant folk living round about in any way she could. Soon, the people got to know and love her. They brought her food, and asked her to pray for them, for they said to one another: "This is a Saint who has come to live among us."

But at last the spring came; the gales were over; the ships began to sail once more. Mildred was thrilled at the thought of being able to go home, but she decided that she had better ask her mother about it first. So she wrote a note to explain, and put in a lock of her hair, and sent it off by the very first boat.

The Queen—or rather, the Abbess—was most surprised and upset when she received the letter.

"Whatever can have happened to the poor child!" she exclaimed, and she sent a ship at once to fetch Mildred home. Then she, and all her novices (there were seventy of them) set off for Ebbsfleet, to meet the ship when it arrived.

(Here I must explain that when the Queen became an

Abbess she changed her name from Ermenburga to Eva or Ebba, and as nuns are sometimes addressed as Domina or Dame, the two words got joined together and she was called Domneva.)

Mildred was delighted when the ship came to fetch her, and from the moment she stepped on board she began to watch for the first sight of home. At last she saw the coast of Thanet, like a faint grey shadow, on the horizon. Nearer and nearer it came. Now she could see the green shore. The ship was actually gliding towards the landing stage. Suddenly, she saw a familiar figure standing there.

" *There's Mother !* " cried Mildred, and without stopping to think, she jumped straight out of the ship on to a big rock which stood up out of the water, and raced along the shore into her mother's arms.

You can see the rock to this day. It is called St. Mildred's rock, and there is a mark on it that is supposed to be her footprint.

" Oh ! Mother, I *am* glad to see you ! " cried Mildred, hugging her.

" Whatever has been happening to you, child ? " asked Domneva, holding her tightly. " I thought you were safe at Chelles."

" I'll tell you everything," answered Mildred happily. " Only, please can I start being a nun at once ? "

" We'll see, my dear," answered her mother, in the kind of tone that mothers use when they really mean yes. " In any case, you shall come back to Minster with me now."

At Minster-in-Thanet, Mildred soon forgot all her troubles. She had to begin learning where she had left off at Chelles and it was hard work to catch up with the others, but she was so pleased to be home that she did not mind how hard she worked, and soon she was ready to be a nun as she wished. Then she and all the other novices took their vows together.

It was not so very long afterwards that Domneva said to her :

" Now, my love, I think it is time you were the Abbess here."

" Oh ! dear," said Mildred, " I don't quite like to think of being above you, Mother."

" Nonsense, dear," answered her mother, " you know that was all arranged long ago."

" Very well," said Mildred, suppressing a sigh. " I think," she added, " that you ought to be Infirmarian, because you are so good at looking after the sick and feeble ones, Mother dear," and so it was arranged.

Now, at last, Mildred was Abbess of Minster-in-Thanet. Calm, gentle, kind and wise, she ruled her nuns well, and won all their hearts.

" I knew she would make a good Abbess," thought her mother fondly.

" So did I," agreed Mildred's Guardian Angel, who happened to be passing. " Oh ! Excuse me—I think she wants me——"

He found Mildred alone in the church with a book in her hand, but quite unable to read, because the place was in darkness.

" Is that you, Guardian Angel dear ? " she asked. " Could you do something about the candles ?   Somebody blew them all out.   I *think* it must have been the devil."

" I shouldn't wonder at all," said the Angel.   " But don't worry, I'll soon put that right," and the next moment the church was full of heavenly light.

I wonder if you have ever been to St. Mildred's Bay for a holiday ? Lots of people do go there, but I don't suppose they ever stop to think how it got its name.

This is how : While Mildred and her nuns were living so peacefully at Minster, England as a whole was anything but peaceful.   At last, the King of Kent (not Egbert, he was dead, but another one named Whitred) decided to call a Council to talk things over, and one of the people asked to come and help was Mildred.   Now, it happened that she went home by ship, and the ship met a storm, and was cast ashore in a bay near Westgate. Ever since that time, it has been called St. Mildred's Bay.

Mildred died at Minster-in-Thanet about the year 700, and was buried in the Abbey Church beside her mother. Afterwards, her relics were taken to SS. Peter, Paul and Augustine's abbey church at Canterbury. She was one of the best loved of all our English Saints, but it was not only in England that the people loved her. Those who had known her when she lived in her little cell in the woods, waiting for a ship to England, never forgot her. They built a church there, and called it St. Mildred's, and to this day the people of that district tell her legends and keep her feast.

VI

SAINT WILFRID—THE WANDERER

Wilfrid's Boyhood

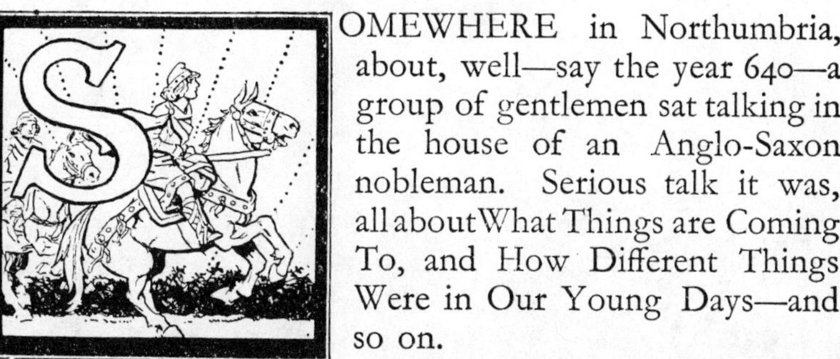

OMEWHERE in Northumbria, about, well—say the year 640—a group of gentlemen sat talking in the house of an Anglo-Saxon nobleman. Serious talk it was, all about What Things are Coming To, and How Different Things Were in Our Young Days—and so on.

Presently, a newcomer joined them. Not a grown-up, but a pretty little boy of about six years old. He was the nobleman's son. He edged his way into the group, and stood leaning against his father's chair, listening gravely to the conversation, his great, solemn eyes fixed first on one face and then on another.

" Hullo ! young man," exclaimed one of the visitors. " What are you after ? A bit young for this sort of conversation, aren't you ? "

His father drew the boy closer to him.

" He likes to hear about these things, don't you, Wilfrid ? " he said.

Wilfrid smiled faintly, for politeness' sake, but said nothing.

" Does he, indeed ! " chuckled another one of the guests. " So it seems ! He'll soon be putting us all right about everything—eh, Wilfrid ? "

The whole party laughed, then went on talking.

Wilfrid did *not* laugh, but went on listening.

He was a happy, friendly little chap, but certainly very serious for his age—this little son of a Saxon nobleman.

None of them saw Saint Michael come.

He loved to listen to the grown-ups talking, and understood a great deal more than anyone would have believed, too. He would puzzle it all out to himself as he listened, deciding who was right, and what he would say if he were grown-up and could join in.   But he was only a little boy, so he kept very quiet, for fear his father would remember about bedtime or something.

Wilfrid was very happy at home until he was twelve years old.   Then he had one of the biggest troubles that anyone can have—his mother died.

This was bad enough, but to make matters worse, his father married again, and his stepmother was terribly unkind to him.

" Now do get out of my way," she would exclaim, almost every time she met him.   Or, " What *are* you doing, Wilfrid ?   Well, whatever it is—*don't*."   Sometimes it was much worse than that.   Beatings, and bread-and-water for practically nothing at all.   Or she would find him some terribly hard work and make him keep at it until he was tired out, and then scold him because he was not quicker.

And always, *always* she made him feel that he was in the way.   That he was not wanted in his own home !

At last, when he was about thirteen, he decided that he could not stand it any longer.   One morning he went to his father and said :

" Father, could I go away, please ? "

" Go away ? " repeated his father.   " For a holiday, do you mean ? "

" No, Father," replied Wilfrid, quietly.   " For good."

There was a silence.   Wilfrid's father felt very uncomfortable, because he knew why the boy wanted to go. He knew about the way his new wife treated his son.   He had tried to protest, but she was a very determined kind of person, and she simply would not take any notice, so in the end he had given it up, and just pretended it was not happening.   (Which is what a lot of us do, I'm afraid, when something wrong is going on and we are not brave enough to fight against it.) But now he could not very well pretend any longer. He said awkwardly :

"Why—er—what's the matter ? "

Wilfrid gave him a long look. He knew that his father understood, but he did not want to cause trouble, so he just said : " I think it will be best, Father."

" Very well," said his father, greatly relieved that his son had not said any more. " Where would you like to go, my boy ? Anywhere you choose——"

" Could I go to Court ? " asked Wilfrid eagerly. Now that the worst was over, he felt quite cheerful, and delighted at the thought of seeing the world. His father, too, was glad, because now he could do something for his son without making his wife angry.

" To Court ? Certainly you shall," he said. " How about being one of the royal pages ? "

" Oh ! yes, I'd like that ! " cried Wilfrid.

" Then I'll see about it at once," his father promised. " You leave it to me, my boy, I'll fix it up in no time."

There was no difficulty about getting Wilfrid a place among the pages of the royal household, for Oswy, King of Northumbria, was one of his father's friends.

A few weeks later, he set off for Bamborough, where the King held his Court. He was wearing a fine new suit, and riding a splendid horse : he had servants to attend him, a trunk bursting with new clothes, and a pocket full of money. He felt pleased and proud and happy.

" A good riddance to bad rubbish ! " said his step-mother, as she watched him ride away.

From the first moment of his arrival at Court, Wilfrid got on splendidly. He soon discovered that many of the nobles there were his father's friends—the very ones who had come to the house when he was little, and to whose talks he had so loved to listen. They were kind to him for his father's sake, did all they could to help him, and introduced him to all the important people at Court, especially to King Oswy, and his wife, Queen Eanfled.

None of this would have been much use, however, if Wilfrid had been an unattractive kind of person, but he was such a nice boy that everyone liked him and was ready to make much of him.

Especially the Queen.

" I *do* like that new page, Wilfrid ! " she exclaimed to the King one day. " He's so bright, and good tempered."

" Yes, he's a nice boy," agreed the King. " Seems to be so full of fun. A handsome lad, too."

" And have you noticed," continued the Queen, " how he always keeps cheerful, whatever happens ? You never see him get all worried and flustered when there is extra work, like the other pages do."

" Seems to regard the whole thing as a great joke," chuckled the King. " Yet he is never rough or wild— which is more than I can say about the others. In fact, in spite of his fun, Wilfrid has a kind of dignity."

" That," said the Queen, " is because he is serious underneath it all. I mean *really* serious. I must have a talk with him. I should like to know what he thinks and feels about things."

Queen Eanfled made a point of getting to know Wilfrid, and he, who still missed his mother a good deal, soon grew very fond of her. She was what his stepmother ought to have been—a second mother to him—and he began to confide in her, and tell her all his hopes and dreams.

One day she said to him :

" And when you are too old to be a page, Wilfrid—I suppose you mean to be a soldier ? "

To her surprise, he answered :

" No, Your Majesty, I want to be something quite different."

" Do you ? " said the Queen, interested, but not greatly surprised, for she had always known that this boy was different from most others. " What do you want, then ? Tell me—you know I will help you if I can."

Wilfrid came to her side. Suddenly, he was very serious.

" I want to be a monk," he said. " Or—or something in the Church."

The Queen looked at him thoughtfully. So young, so handsome, so popular ! And he wanted to leave the world where he was almost certain to make a great name for himself, and be a monk !

" Are you quite sure, Wilfrid ? " she asked.

" Quite," he answered firmly. " I've thought about it for a long time. I want to work for God and His Church all my life."

They talked it over a little more, and as soon as she was quite certain that this really was the life Wilfrid wanted, the Queen undertook to help him.

She began by persuading the King to let him off the military training which all the royal pages had to go through, and send him instead to school at the Monastery on the Island of Lindisfarne (now called Holy Island). She hated to part from him, but she knew that if he was to do well in the life he had chosen he ought to begin training at once. So it was arranged that he should go to Lindisfarne as attendant upon an old noble named Cudda, who, ill and tired, wanted to leave the Court and end his life as a monk in this famous monastery.

The island lies just off the coast of Northumberland. One fine morning, they set off for it together, the old nobleman and the young page. One had almost the whole of his life, the other had only a tiny little bit, but what they had each wanted to give with both hands to God.

Doubts and Difficulties

WILFRID settled down quite happily at Lindisfarne. There were a good many other boys there—all studying to be priests—and he enjoyed working with them.

But there was one question which he kept turning over and over in his mind the whole time.

He had first come up against it when he went to Court. He found that, though they were both Christians, the King and Queen each had their own priests, who held separate services for them, and actually kept the great festival of Easter at different times.

He asked one of his father's friends about it.

" It is because Her Majesty belongs to the Roman Church, and His Majesty to the Celtic Church," this gentleman explained. " They are a little different in some ways."

" I see," said Wilfrid, thoughtfully. " Is that why the Queen's chaplain has his hair shaved differently from the King's. And why they don't keep Easter together ? "

" That's it."

" Oh ! " said Wilfrid. " Thank you."

He did not think much more about it at the time, except to decide that, as the Queen was so kind to him, he should belong to her Church.

What was his surprise, then, to find, when he got to Lindisfarne, that there, where the Queen herself had sent him, they did everything in the Celtic way.

" This *is* puzzling ! " sighed Wilfrid.

Perhaps you find it puzzling too, but it's quite simple really.

This is what happened : Christianity first came to Britain with the Romans. Then the Romans went away, and the Danes, Angles and Saxons came. They were pagans. They drove the Celtic peoples into Wales and Ireland, and Christianity with them. Britain became pagan again.

But not for long.   Soon, the great Saint Columba came from Ireland with his monks, to preach the gospel to the people of Scotland and Northern England.   He taught them the ways of the old Celtic Church which had been handed down from the time of the Romans, but as a matter of fact, some changes had been made since those times. One was about the way the monks should shave their heads, but the really important one was the date of Easter. These changes came from Rome, and because the whole Christian Church was guided from Rome, they were made everywhere.

Except in Britain.   The people of the British Isles, being cut off from the Continent by the sea, knew nothing whatever about these changes so they went on just as before.

Now, after a while there came another great Saint— Saint Augustine, to preach to the people of England.   He landed in the south, and as he came straight from Rome, he naturally brought the new Roman ways with him.   And as time went on, Augustine's monks worked northwards and Columba's monks worked southward, until they met in the middle.   Then things became difficult, for one group belonged to the Roman Church and the other belonged to the Celtic Church, and both were quite sure that they were right.

After thinking all this over very carefully, Wilfrid came to the conclusion that the Celtic Church was rather old-fashioned, and the Roman way was right, but there were still a lot of things he did not understand, and so, when he was about seventeen, and had been at Lindisfarne four years, he decided he would go to Rome and learn all about them.

Again the Queen helped.   He was too young, she said, to go all that way alone, but he might go as far as Canterbury, where her cousin, King Erconbert of Kent, ruled. There he must wait until some older person was travelling to Rome, and they could go together.

He had to wait a year, but at last he heard of a nobleman

named Baducing, who was going to Rome, and arranged to travel with him.

(This nobleman, by the way, is usually known as Benedict Biscop, and it was he who founded the monasteries of Wearmouth and Jarrow, where the Venerable Bede lived.)

Well, they set off for Rome. On the way, they stopped at Lyons, and stayed with the Prince Bishop Delphinus.

A Prince Bishop rules over certain lands like a Prince, beside being a Bishop.

Delphinus took a great fancy to Wilfrid. He even suggested that Wilfrid should marry one of his nieces instead of being a priest. " You shall have my favourite one," said he, " and I will leave you some of my lands to rule over when I die."

But Wilfrid refused. " You see I really *want* to be a priest," he explained.

" Oh ! " said Delphinus. " Oh ! well, of course, if you're *sure*, I suppose that settles it."

However, Wilfrid stayed at Lyons for a whole year, leaving Benedict Biscop to go on to Rome alone.

At the end of the year he continued his journey, and reached great Rome at last. One of the first things he did when he arrived was to go up to the Monastery of St. Andrew's to pray. He prayed for power and understanding to teach others. Then he set about looking for someone to teach *him*.

He found Archbishop Boniface, Secretary to the Pope. Boniface kept a school in his house for young men who wanted to be priests. Wilfrid joined it, and there he learned exactly how things were done in the Roman Church, and why. Then he started for home, eager to teach what he had learned to the English people.

On the way back he again stopped at Lyons, to see the Prince Bishop Delphinus, and there he stayed for another three years. It seems a very long time, but he and the Bishop were great friends, and I daresay Delphinus kept saying, " Oh ! do stay a bit longer."

That visit very nearly cost him his life, though, for while he was there, the Queen of France, who was a pagan, and simply hated Christians, suddenly had Delphinus arrested. "If," she said, "he will insist on being a Christian, he had better be a dead one," and she ordered him to be killed.

In spite of having tried to persuade Wilfrid not to be a priest, Delphinus was a brave man and a true Christian, and he would not give in. So he died a martyr, and Wilfrid, who went with him to the place of his martyrdom, very nearly did the same. Indeed, the Queen was just about to give the order, when someone explained that he was an Englishman.

"*English?*" exclaimed the Queen. "Oh! for goodness sake leave him alone then, or we shall have trouble with those Islanders."

So Wilfrid was saved. He stayed only long enough to bury his friend Delphinus. Then he returned to England.

An Important Meeting

HINGS had been happening while Wilfrid was away. To begin with, the King's son, Prince Alchfrid, had been given the southern part of the kingdom to look after, and was now ruling it as a sort of under-king to his father. When Wilfrid was a page, he and Alchfrid were great friends, so the Prince was very glad to see Wilfrid back, especially as he, too, belonged to the Roman Church, and had been having rather a difficult time, trying to persuade all his people to do the same.

"I *am* glad to see you," he told Wilfrid. "We're all feeling dreadfully worried. Some want the Roman way and some the Celtic way. Those who want to keep to the old Celtic way just will not be persuaded, while the others want the whole thing changed over to the Roman way *at once* without giving the old-fashioned ones a chance to get used to the idea."

" But you believe in the Roman way, don't you, Alchfrid ? " asked Wilfrid quickly.

" Of course I do," the Prince replied. " That's the way my mother taught me and I want to see it the same all over Northumbria, so if you've come home to teach it to the people I'll help you all I can. Only," he sighed, " you'd never believe what a lot of trouble it's causing."

The trouble went on and on, until at last King Oswy said : " Look here, we simply must decide something definite. We are all one church really and we all agree about the very important things, so there's no earthly reason why we shouldn't come to an agreement about Easter and all those other points. Listen, we'll have a meeting, and some from each side shall come to it. Then, first, we'll ask God to help us to see which is really right, and then we'll talk it over. And whatever we decide there —so it shall be."

The meeting was held at the Monastery of Streaneshalch, which is the place we now call Whitby, and the Chairman was not a man at all, but a woman—the Abbess Hilda— Saint Hilda she is now. This was not so surprising as it sounds, because there were many women in high places in the Church in those days, and Hilda, who was Abbess of the Monastery in which the meeting was held, was one of them. She was a wise, calm person, and had had a lot of practice in ruling both men and women, and I have no doubt she made a very good chairman indeed.

Beside the Abbess Hilda, there was of course King Oswy and Queen Eanfled, and their son, Prince Alchfrid ; and there was Agilbert, Bishop of the West Saxons, who had just ordained Wilfrid a priest, and some other bishops and priests, and of course Wilfrid himself. Wilfrid led the ones that wanted the Roman way, and Colman, Bishop of Lindisfarne, led the others. And as some spoke the old

British language and some Anglo-Saxon, a dear old Bishop named Cedd, who understood both, acted as interpreter.

Well, the meeting began. First, the King spoke. He said : " Since we all serve the same God, we ought all to do it in the same way, and have the same rules, and keep the festivals all together.   So the best thing to do is to find out which is the right way and then all keep to that." And everybody said : " Hear ! Hear ! " and " God Save the King."

But it is much easier to say " let us agree " than it is to do so. There was a great deal of argument, and some people got rather excited, but at last the King came to the conclusion that as all the Christians in the world except a small group in these islands followed the Roman rules, it would be better for them also to do so. Which, seeing that he himself had been brought up in the Celtic Church, was very fair and sensible on his part.

So it was agreed, and the meeting broke up. Some of the monks from Lindisfarne were dreadfully upset, and Bishop Colman would not stay there, but went straight back to Iona.

But Wilfrid was pleased : and when Prince Alchfrid made him head of a fine new monastery at Ripon, he was still more pleased.

However, before he had had time to settle down there properly, a still more important position was offered to him. That of Bishop of York. There had been no Bishop there for some time, and as the Bishop who ruled Lindisfarne after Colman left had just died, it was decided that it would be a good idea for Wilfrid to be Bishop of York and rule the Church all over Northumbria.

Of course, before he could do this he had to be consecrated Bishop, and he was so anxious that this should be done in the right way, that he went all the way to Compiegne in France, in order that his friend Agilbert, who was now Bishop of Paris, should do it.

It was a very splendid ceremony—almost too splendid, for it seems to have made Wilfrid forget the work he was really supposed to do. For he did a very strange thing. Instead of going home to start his new work, he settled down where he was, and for two whole years the new Bishop of York remained in France.

Wandering and Homecoming

NATURALLY, the people of Northumbria were worried about it. " But when is he coming home ? " they asked each other, as the time went by. " The Bishop of York should be *in* York. Or, at least, in Northumbria. To stay a few months, perhaps, yes, we understand that, but all this time ! No, no, it won't do. It really will not do."

At last they sent a deputation to King Oswy, begging him to make someone else Bishop of York, because they really could not wait for Wilfrid any longer.

" I see your point," said the King, thoughtfully. " Yes, I quite see your point. Well—I suppose I had better choose someone else then."

He chose the Abbot Chad of Lastingham, and he was made Bishop of York. " He is, perhaps, not such a great man as Wilfrid," said the people, " but at least he is *here*."

When Wilfrid came home at last and found what had happened he was terribly disappointed, and rather indignant, though really it was his own fault.

" But *I* am Bishop of York," he declared.

" I'm sorry," said the King, " but you see you were so long away, and we had to have somebody.   No, I'm afraid I can't do anything about it.   It wouldn't be fair to Bishop Chad to turn him out now, would it ? "

" N—no," agreed Wilfrid reluctantly.   " I suppose not. But I do think you might have let me know first."

There was nothing for it but to go back to Ripon, for he was still Abbot of the Monastery there, and that is what he did.

For three years he carried on with his work at Ripon, trying hard not to think of York. It was very difficult, because he was full of plans, and had all manner of wonderful ideas for making the Church in England great and splendid, if only he had the chance.

Then, at the end of the three years, the chance came. The Archbishop of Canterbury, who knew really that the work at York was too much for Bishop Chad, and that Wilfrid was the right man for it, arranged that Chad should go with some monks who were travelling to the Kingdom of Mercia as missionaries, while Wilfrid came to York, to be Bishop, as he should have been from the first.

Bishop Chad did not mind, for he had never wanted to hold such a high position, and he much preferred to be a missionary.

As for Wilfrid, he was delighted. Now, at last he could begin the work he had been longing to do.   And he did do it, well and truly. He was particularly good at building beautiful churches. He had some wonderful ideas, and some of the churches he built are the finest in England.   For one, at Ripon, he brought workmen all the way from Italy, to build in the Italian style, and on the altar there he placed a golden box studded with jewels, containing a copy of the gospels written in letters of gold on purple vellum : in another—York Minster—he actually put real glass windows, a thing which many people had never even seen before : a third—at Hexham—was said to be the finest church on this side of the Alps.

He was working away, happy and busy, and everything seemed to be going splendidly, when suddenly a new difficulty arose. The Archbishop of Canterbury announced that the part of England over which Wilfrid ruled was too large for one, so it had better be divided into four. Wilfrid was to keep one part, and three new Bishops would be chosen for the others.

Wilfrid did not like this idea at all. He declared that the Archbishop had no right to do it, and when the Archbishop insisted, he went off to Rome to see the Pope about it.

He meant to go straight across to France, but before he set out, word came to him that his enemies had hatched a plot to seize him in France and keep him prisoner, so that he could not go to the Pope.

Wilfrid considered. It might be all nonsense. On the other hand, it might not. Better be on the safe side, he thought. He decided he would not land in France, but in Friesland, and go to Rome that way.

Friesland is now part of Holland. Wilfrid arrived there in the depth of winter, to find all the roads blocked with snow. It was impossible to get any further. There was nothing to do but settle down and wait for the spring.

He did not waste his time while he was waiting. It happened that the Frieslanders spoke a language so much like Anglo-Saxon that they and Wilfrid could understand each other quite well. So he spent the winter preaching to them, for they were pagans, and by the time the flowers were springing up in the woods of Friesland, Christianity was springing up in the hearts of its people. Then Wilfrid said good-bye to them and continued his journey.

When the Pope heard about the Archbishop's idea for the three new bishops, he decided that Wilfrid was right about it. He ought to remain head of the Church all over Northumbria, but if the Archbishop of Canterbury thought there was too much for one person to do, he might choose some other Bishops to work *under* Wilfrid.

Wilfrid went back to England triumphant, but his triumph did not last long, for in spite of what the Pope said the Archbishop of Canterbury insisted on keeping to his own plan. By this time King Oswy and Queen Eanfled were both dead, and Prince Alchfrid too, and the new King and Queen, Egfrid and Ermenburga, agreed with the Archbishop. This was bad enough, but there was worse to come, for, because he still would not agree, Wilfrid was arrested and clapped into prison for rebellion. There he might have stayed for the rest of his life, had not the King's Aunt, the Abbess Ebba of Coldingham, persuaded the King to set him free.

Now, all these ups and downs had taken a good many years, and when Wilfrid at last came out of prison he was growing old, and very tired. When he found that, during his imprisonment, his own people had been turning against him, so that instead of welcoming him back, they greeted him with coldness, hatred, and even threats to his life, he felt that he just could not struggle any longer. He left Northumbria, and after seeking refuge first in one place and then in another, came at last to the Kingdom of the South Saxons, which we call Sussex now. There he found rest and a home, for though the people were pagans their King was a Christian.

After a time, when he had got over his journey, he began to feel he would like to preach the gospel to these folk who, though they were not Christians, were behaving more like them than some folks who were. Then he thought, " No. I am here as a refugee. I mustn't seem to be forcing new ideas upon them as soon as I arrive. I'll just do anything I can to help them in a general sort of way until we know each other better. Then, perhaps——"

As it happened, the South Saxons were in great need of help just then, for there had been a long drought, and it looked as if there would soon be a famine. Nothing would grow in the fields : there was no grass for the cattle to feed upon. The people were in despair.

" But, good gracious ! " exclaimed Wilfrid, " what

about the fish? You've still got the *sea*. There's plenty of fish there to feed you all until better times come."

He was talking to a little group of the common people, but his suggestion did not seem to cheer them up in the least.

"We've caught them all," said one man, gloomily. "Might be one or two more left perhaps, but——"

"*You've caught all the fish in the sea !*" gasped Wilfrid. "But that's impossible !"

The people nodded their heads silently.

"There aren't many, you know," explained one of the women.

"Not many ?" Wilfrid did not know what to make of this. "Here—come along down to the shore," said he, "and show me what you mean. There is some mystery here."

They led him to the water's edge. One of the men took a tiny eel net and, wading a little way into the water, cast it in and brought it up again—empty. "You see ?" he said. "I tell you we've *eaten* them all !"

"But—but don't you fish from boats ?" cried Wilfrid. "Far out, where the water is deep, and the real fish live ?"

The people gaped at him. "Fish from boats ?" they said vaguely.

They had lived near the coast all that time, but it had never occurred to them to go out on the sea and fish. All they had done was to wade about at the edge, catching eels !

"Oh ! come along," said Wilfrid, briskly, as soon as he realised the situation. "I'll soon show you how to get a meal."

Long ago, when he had been at school at Lindisfarne, he had learnt how to make both boats and nets : how to sail the one and cast the other. Full of enthusiasm, he now set to work to teach these people how to do the same. They learnt quickly, for hunger was behind them, and as for Wilfrid, he was happier, working with these simple people, than ever he had been struggling with the Archbishop of Canterbury.

F

It was not long before, in newly-made boats, with great fishing nets made from the little eel nets fastened together, the South Saxons set out on their first fishing trip. When they returned, their boats loaded with fish—enough and to spare for all the hungry people, what joy, what excitement there was !

No wonder the people listened gladly to Wilfrid when later he began to tell them the story of Our Lord. He became their Bishop, and soon he was baptising great numbers of them. Then, just as he had baptised a specially large group, the rain fell, and the drought was over.

To show his gratitude to Wilfrid, the King of the South Saxons gave him that bit of land running into the sea not far from Chichester called Selsey Bill, and there he built a monastery and a church. Then a nobleman of the country gave him a great part of the Isle of Wight, where still the people were pagans, so that it seemed as if Wilfrid might have settled down and made his home among the South Saxons.

But just then came a message from the Archbishop of Canterbury calling him home to Northumbria, to be Abbot of Ripon and Bishop of York again. So Wilfrid sent a nephew of his who was a priest to convert the Isle of Wight people, and he went back to York, hoping that at last his troubles were over.

So they were for a time. Then the old quarrels began again. The King and the Archbishop declared that Wilfrid was trying to get too much power for himself, so Wilfrid went off again to Rome to see the Pope. But by this time he was ill, and seemed to have lost all his fighting spirit, so, although the Pope again said he was in the right, he could not bear the thought of going back to England, for he felt that only enemies awaited him there. He begged to be allowed to stay for the rest of his life in Rome, but the Pope said no. His work was in England and he must go back to it.

Feeling terribly tired and sad, Wilfrid obeyed, but he had not gone far when he was taken so ill that he had to be carried in a litter.   He got as far as Meaux, in France, and there he had to stop, for he was so ill that his friends thought he was going to die.

But they were wrong.   Much to everyone's surprise, he recovered, and managed to get safely back to England.

" I've another four years to live yet," he told his friends. " Yes—I am quite certain.   You see, while I lay ill at Meaux I had a visitor.   The Archangel Michael.   Yes, indeed !   He told me that your prayers and tears had saved my life, but that he would come back for me in four years' time.   So you see, I *know*."

Wilfrid was too ill to be Bishop of York again, but he was made Bishop of Hexham, which was much smaller, and not such hard work, and beside that he was still Abbot of Ripon.   He did not mind.   He knew he had nearly finished his work, and he just wanted to go along quietly for the rest of the time.

He spent his days very peacefully, mostly in reading the gospels, and praying.   But he still longed for Rome, and when the four years were nearly up he decided to try to reach his beloved city, so that he might die there.   He was really much too ill to travel, but he would go.   At the end of September, 709, he started, with some of his monks, but they only got as far as Oundle in Northamptonshire, for he simply could not go any further.   So they took him to a monastery near by, and there he died.

It was on October 3rd that he called his friends to him, and said smiling :

" I am expecting the Archangel Michael to-day.   Will you sing to me, while I am waiting for him ? "

They sang the one hundred and fourth psalm, and by the time they had finished singing Wilfrid was no longer with them.   None of them saw Saint Michael come, but they said afterwards that they heard, above their own voices, a sound like the singing of birds . . . or angels.

"I am no man's Leader," said Guthlac, "but God's servant."

VII

SAINT GUTHLAC—MAN
OF FUTURE GLORY

The Sign in the Sky

HERE was great excitement when St. Guthlac was born. There usually is a good deal over a new baby, but this was a special *kind* of excitement.

Guthlac's father was Penwald, a rich nobleman of Mercia, who had married a fair and noble lady named Tette, in the days when Ethelred was King of the Mercians. Mercia was a big kingdom right in the middle of England.

But about this excitement. Well, one night a woman who lived near Penwald's house was standing at her window when she noticed a glow in the sky, almost as though a house was on fire. She leaned out, trying to see where it came from—then gave an excited cry and rushed from the room and downstairs to the front door, nearly colliding with her sister who was coming from another part of the house.

" Do be careful, Edyth," said her sister, rather crossly. " Whatever is the matter ? "

" I don't know—something marvellous," answered Edyth, flinging open the door and rushing into the street. " I saw something——"

" Saw what ? " questioned her sister, following her. " What *is* it ? "

Edyth was gazing intently at the sky.

" I saw a hand," she whispered. " A red hand, holding a golden cross. Look—there it is ! "

77

"Nonsense," her sister answered tartly, "I see nothing. You are always imagining things."

Just at that moment, a group of men and women came hurrying past.

"Did you see it?" asked one of the men. "A hand in the sky, holding a cross of gold."

"There you are!" exclaimed Edyth. "Yes, I saw it," she continued, speaking to the man. "What does it mean, do you think?"

"We can't imagine," the man answered, "but it must be something important."

"Do come on," urged another man in the crowd, impatiently. "The sign might vanish."

The whole group began to move on again.

"We are going to try to trace the house at which it is pointing," cried the first man, over his shoulder.

Edyth caught up her skirts and ran after them.

"Edyth!" called her sister. "Where are you going? *Edyth!*"

But Edyth was already running down the street after the others.

By this time great numbers of people were coming from all sides. "The sign—the sign," they asked each other, "which way is it pointing?"

Suddenly Edyth cried:

"Look! It is over the Lord Penwald's house!" Everyone rushed in that direction.

The house was dark and silent. "There! Look," whispered Edyth to a woman beside her. "Can you see it? A red hand, holding a cross of gold? It's pointing straight to the house. Ah! now it's gone."

A long sigh ran through the crowd. First one and then another fell on his knees. Soon all were kneeling there in the dark. Someone began to pray that God would show them the meaning of the sign.

Suddenly, a light streamed from the door of Penwald's house. A woman ran out to the kneeling people.

"It's all right!" she cried, excitedly. "There's nothing

to fear.   Keep up your hearts, for a Man of Future Glory is born on this earth ! "

" A Man of Future Glory ! "   The people talked it over all the way home.   There were so many different *kinds* of glory.   Next day the story was all over the district.   In a week it was all over Mercia ; in a month, all over England.

Meanwhile, the " Man of Future Glory " lay cuddled in his mother's arms, placidly sucking his thumb.

" Future Glory or not," remarked his father Penwald, " he is certainly the finest baby I have ever seen."

" Of course he is," agreed Tette.   " Let's call him Guthlac."

The Still, Small Voice

GUTHLAC grew from the dearest little baby to a most charming little boy—sharp as a needle and bright as a button, with a nature sweet as a May morning.

" You mark my words, Madam," remarked his nurse to Tette, " that child is just brimful of goodness. *Future glory*, did I say ? Why, you can see it shining in his face already, bless him ! "

It was not only the nurse—everyone who knew little Guthlac said the same. So they were particularly disappointed when, as he grew into his 'teens, he changed completely.

When anyone is exceptionally strong, healthy and clever, they need a great deal to do to keep them out of mischief. Whether it is good or whether it is bad, they simply must be doing *something*. I think it was probably just this that was the matter with Guthlac. He absolutely had to use up the energy that was boiling and bubbling inside him, and so, since he was too young to find the right things to do with it, he did the wrong ones.

What he did was to gather a crowd of boys about his own age (he could only have been about fifteen) and form them into a kind of gang with himself as captain. The gang roamed all over Mercia, burning, stealing, killing. If they had a grudge against anyone, they would take revenge, as they called it (no matter who was in the wrong really). Up and down the country they roamed, idle, reckless, cruel, bringing trouble wherever they went, and Guthlac—Guthlac, for whom God had sent a special sign when he was born—Guthlac was their leader ! No wonder people were disappointed. " The Man of Future Glory," they said, has turned out a " Man of Present Shame." His father was angry : his mother upset : those who had seen the hand in the sky were puzzled : those who had not said, " I told you so ! "

For nine years this went on. Guthlac pretended to himself that he was having a fine time, but he wasn't really, because, no matter how loudly he shouted or how fiercely he fought, he had a horrid feeling inside all the time—as though a large, cold stone were lying where his heart should be—and that spoilt it all.

However, he would not take any notice, but just went on behaving more and more wildly, until suddenly he changed again.

It was one night when he and his gang had just finished what they called an " Expedition." That is to say, they had burnt a number of houses (first stealing everything valuable inside them), killed a great many harmless and innocent people, and driven the rest to wander homeless in the woods. Altogether, as the gang agreed, it had been a most successful affair. Tired out with the day's work, they were sleeping round their camp fire. All, that is, but Guthlac.

That night, Guthlac could not sleep.

He lay on his back on the hillside where he and his men had made their camp. Below, he could still see the smoke rising from the houses they had burnt. Staring harder, he thought he could make out a few people searching forlornly for what was left of their belongings.

"I *must* go to sleep," he muttered feverishly.

But he could not. He could only lie there with that terribly wide-awake feeling which always comes when you are longing to sleep, and cannot.

Have you ever had something tremendously important to say to someone, and found that he would not stop to listen, but would keep rushing about just *doing* things? That was the trouble with Guthlac. He was so busy shouting, stealing, and fighting, never still and never quiet, that he gave himself no chance to hear what God was trying to say to him. And that was a pity, because He had something very important to say. However, on this particular night, Guthlac had actually stopped dashing about, and was still: he had stopped shouting, and was ready to listen. That was just what God had been waiting for.

What He said to Guthlac, only Guthlac knows, but suddenly everything seemed to him different. It was like coming up into the sunlight when you have been living in a dark cellar: it was like being able to hear the birds instead of a brass band that never stops. It was just the difference between hating and loving. All at once, Guthlac found that the horrible " cold stone " feeling inside was gone. He did not want to hurt people any more, but to help them: he did not want to hate people any longer—he loved them—and God most of all. With a big sigh of happiness he turned on his side and fell into a delicious sleep.

He woke to that glorious feeling—something splendid

has happened! Just for a moment he wondered what it was. Then he remembered—of course—everything was different now.

"Yes," said he to himself, sitting up, "that's all very fine, Guthlac, my lad, but what are you going to *do* about it?" He glanced across at his companions. They were still asleep. It was not yet day. He must make up his mind before the others woke.

Then, for the first time for nine years, Guthlac began to *think*. He thought and thought, as he lay there, how to turn the helping and loving feeling into action. The point about a feeling is that it is meant to lead to doing. (It would be no use feeling like giving someone a present, unless you actually went and bought one, would it?) So Guthlac thought and thought and at last he remembered how he had heard of kings of old who had given up their thrones and gone away to be monks or hermits, so that they might serve God with all their hearts and minds.

"That's what I'll do!" he exclaimed, and he vowed that if God would let him live until the morning he would be His servant for the rest of his life.

He did not sleep again, but lay waiting quietly until his companions should wake. Soon, the sun rose. One after another the sleeping young men wakened. As soon as they were all awake, Guthlac rose and called them to him.

They came crowding round, expecting orders for some fresh "Expedition." Instead:

"Boys," said Guthlac, "I want you to find a new leader. I can lead you no longer."

They stared at him in astonishment. Then all began speaking at once.

"But why?" "What's the matter?" "What has happened?" "Have *we* done anything?"

"No, no," Guthlac assured them, "I'm not complaining. It's true that we've all been behaving shamefully, but that's chiefly my fault. No, it's——"

"Ah!" interrupted one of the gang, "I suppose

you've found something that pays you better. Got a new idea that you mean to keep to yourself, eh ? "

Guthlac smiled. " Well, yes, in a way," he admitted.

" I thought as much ! " snarled the other. " Well, let me tell you——"

" No," said Guthlac firmly, " let *me* tell *you*." He waited until there was silence. Then : " From to-day," said he, " I am no man's leader, but God's servant. I am going away to be a monk—or at least, to try."

The gang were thunderstruck. They did not like the idea at all, for Guthlac was a very good leader. Beside, some of them really were fond of him.

" Oh ! look here," they clamoured, " you can't do that ! " " I say, you know, you can't desert the gang." " Now, do be a good fellow and say you'll still be our chief."

Guthlac shook his head. " It's nice of you to want me," he said, " but I've made up my mind."

Still they begged him. " Think it over," they said. " Do think it over."

" I have," said Guthlac, and nothing would shake him.

From that day, he left the gang for ever. Then, having said good-bye to parents and friends, he turned his back on everything he had ever known, and set off to begin the new life he had chosen.

He was only twenty-four.

A New Beginning

"'VE got to begin again, right from the beginning," decided Guthlac. "But where?" He came to the conclusion to go to Repton. At Repton there was what was called a double monastery, one house for monks and another for nuns, all ruled over by an Abbess. So to Repton went Guthlac, and there he settled down to learn to be a monk.

At first the other monks did not like him very much. They thought he was showing off, because he would not eat meat or drink wine, and was altogether terribly stern with himself. But when they got to know him better, and found how cheerful and patient he was, and not at all the showing-off kind, they changed their minds, and in the end they grew very fond of him.

For two years he stayed at Repton, learning all the psalms, hymns and prayers, in fact, everything that a monk has to know, and trying all the time to be as good as possible. But still he did not feel quite satisfied. Gradually, he came to the conclusion that what he really wanted was to go away to some very wild and desolate place where there was not even a monastery. Somewhere where he could listen to God—and talk to Him, too—without anyone or anything to interrupt.

He went to see the Abbess about it.

"Well, my son," she said, "what is it?"

"It's like this, Reverend Mother," began Guthlac, "I've been thinking—of course, it's very nice here, and everyone is very kind, but I—I feel I would like to be by myself more. If I could live alone, in some wild and desolate place——"

"I see," said the Abbess. "You would like to be a hermit."

" That's it, Reverend Mother," cried Guthlac eagerly. " That is what I should like more than anything."

" We will consider it, my son," said the Abbess. " If you really wish to leave us, I think you may be permitted to go."

So it was decided. Guthlac was given permission to leave the monastery and become a hermit.

He was delighted. He began to pester everyone with the question—" Do you know a good place for a Hermitage ? "

At last someone mentioned the Fen District.

" Ah ! " said one of the monks, " you can't do better than try the Fens."

" Are they really wild ? " insisted Guthlac. " Wild and desolate. Not a lot of people ? "

" People ! " exclaimed the monk. " People, indeed ! Why, there's nothing there. Absolutely nothing."

" That ought to be wild and desolate enough, certainly," said Guthlac. " Thank you for telling me. I'll go and have a look round there to-morrow."

Next day he set off for the Fens. We still have a Fen Country in Cambridgeshire and Lincolnshire, but the marshes have been drained, crops planted and towns built. In Guthlac's time the Fens were just miles and miles of marsh, with deep, sluggish streams crossing them, sometimes broadening out into lakes of dark, gloomy-looking water, in which grew great clumps of reeds and osiers. Only here and there were islands of firm ground on which it was possible to live.

" This looks the right kind of place," said Guthlac to himself. He was only on the edge of the real Fens, but already it began to look more wild and desolate than any country he had ever seen. He began to ask the few people he met if they knew of a good place for a hermit. At last he met a man named Tatwin.

" Yes," said he, in answer to Guthlac's question, " I know exactly the place you want—only you *won't* want it when you see it."

" Why not ? " demanded Guthlac.   " What's the matter with it."

" Too wild," said Tatwin gloomily.

" But I want it wild," said Guthlac.   " What else is the matter with it ? "

" Too lonely," said Tatwin.

" But I like to be lonely," replied Guthlac.   " Anything else ? "

" Yes," said Tatwin. " There are the horrors."

" What do you mean—horrors ? " asked Guthlac. " What kind of horrors ? "

Tatwin shook his head gloomily. " I don't know what kind," he said, " but I do know that everyone who has ever tried to live there has had to give it up on account of the horrors."

" But I was told that the Fens were so wild that there was absolutely *nothing* there," protested Guthlac.

" There isn't," answered Tatwin.   " Only the horrors."

" Well, I'd like to look at this place, anyhow," decided Guthlac.   " Could you take me there ? I don't suppose any horrors will come while we're just looking round."

Tatwin agreed and went off to get his boat, for the place of which he had spoken was an island.   Soon he was rowing Guthlac along one of the dark, slowly-moving streams that crossed the Fens.   The further they went, the wilder and more desolate it became.

At last Tatwin turned his boat, and, crashing through a great clump of reeds, brought it to the shore of a little island known as Crowland or Croyland.

" This is it," said he.

Guthlac stepped ashore.   " Well," said he slowly, as he looked about him, " I should never have dreamed of there being such a place.   It's certainly lonely enough."

" Nobody knows about it but me," said Tatwin, rather proudly.

" It looks to me as if it will be the very place I want," said Guthlac.   " Let's have a good look round."

Tatwin had brought food, and there were plenty of

fish, so they decided to stay a few days and explore the island.

"Well," said Tatwin, when they had seen everything. "Allowing for the horrors—will it do?"

"It will do splendidly," Guthlac assured him. He was quite excited about it.

"You're *sure* you are allowing for the horrors?" said Tatwin.

Guthlac laughed. "Oh! bother the horrors!" he said. "God will be here, too, won't He? Well, then!"

They had one more good look round, so that Guthlac could decide exactly what he should need in order to settle there. Then Tatwin rowed back to the point from which they had started, for Guthlac wanted to return to Repton to collect his things. Besides, he had not said good-bye to anyone properly.

They were all very pleased to see him back, and eager to hear all about the place he had found. He stayed there three months, for there was a great deal to do, but at last everything was ready. Then he said good-bye to his friends, and taking with him only two servants, set off to begin his new life at Croyland.

The Hermitage in the Fens

AT first they were all very busy getting settled.   To begin with, they had to build a house.   There was an old burial mound made by the Ancient Britons, with a water cistern near by, and here Guthlac built his hermitage, and a little church beside it.   Then there was the ground to clear so that they could plant some barley for food—and, oh! a great many other things to attend to.

However, at last it was all finished.   Clothed in skins, living only on barley bread and water—it does not sound very pleasant.   But Guthlac was happier than he had ever been before.

And then the trouble began.

One night, while he was saying his prayers, a host of fierce, wild creatures swooped down upon him.   They dragged him from his house, threw him into the fen water, fished him out again, then pushed him among the prickliest brambles they could find.   As he crawled out they stood around him, waving great clubs and shouting :

" Go away !   Be off with you !   This place belongs to us."

" Not at all," said Guthlac calmly.   " This place, like all other places, belongs to God.   I shall not leave unless He tells me to."

" If you don't go," shouted a frightfully ugly person with a perfectly enormous club, " we shall do far worse things to you than we have done to-night ! "

" Well, I shan't go," replied Guthlac firmly, " whatever you do."

Luckily the dawn came then, so they left him.

" Whew ! What a night ! " said Guthlac to himself as he walked rather shakily back to his house.   " So those are the horrors Tatwin spoke of ! What were they, I wonder ? Demons ? Or some of those British who used to live in these islands before we came ? Not nice neighbours, anyhow.   Not nice neighbours at all."

Some nights later, the " neighbours " came again. Guthlac was wakened from sleep by the sound of a great number of people talking. They were speaking in British which he understood because he had once lived among the British people for a time. He rose and peeped out. Yes —there they were. He could clearly see the frightfully ugly one with the enormous club. They were Ancient Britons who had taken refuge on the island when the Angles and Saxons invaded Britain, and they were afraid that Guthlac meant to drive them from this, their only home. That was why they attacked him.

This time they did not drag him out of his house—they simply set fire to it, and when Guthlac managed to get out they attacked him with spears. But he was not a bit afraid, and began to sing a psalm at the top of his voice, whereupon the Britons, quite unable to make anything of this way of fighting, slunk off, and that was the last he saw of them.

His next danger came, not from enemies, but from one he had counted a friend.

A priest named Beccel had asked to be allowed to join him on the island, promising to be his servant and to obey him in everything. Guthlac agreed and for a time things went quite well.

Then Beccel began to get jealous. He saw that Guthlac was getting quite well known. Important people were coming to visit him. Everyone looked up to him. Every- one said how wise and good he was. In fact, he was becoming a famous hermit.

" I wish I were a famous hermit," thought Beccel enviously. " Fancy if all those important people came to see me. . . . I don't see why they shouldn't . . . really. If Brother Guthlac weren't here, I dare say they *would* come to see me. If he died, for instance. . . ."

So it went on all day and most of the night. Round and round inside Beccel's head the thoughts kept running— " If Brother Guthlac were to die I could be the famous hermit. If Brother Guthlac were to die——"

G

Then, one morning, while he was shaving Guthlac, the next thought came—"*Why shouldn't I kill him?*" He paused in his work, his heart beating furiously. Here was a marvellous chance! He had a weapon ready in his hand! The words began again, "If Brother Guthlac were to die, I could be——"

"Why are you entertaining those devils of temptation, Brother Beccel?" asked Guthlac quietly.

Beccel jumped—then began to tremble. He turned red and then white, and started to stammer something.

"Hush!" said Guthlac. "Won't you spit out this poison? I can see you are tempted, but you just turn away from the devil's teaching."

At that, Beccel fell in a heap at his feet and burst into tears.

"Oh! how *awful* I am!" he sobbed. "I've been so jealous—I wanted to kill you so that I could be the famous hermit—just as if I *could*! Oh! dear, how frightfully wicked I am—you'll never forgive me—I know you won't——"

Guthlac patted his shoulder comfortingly.

"There! there!" he said, "it's all right. Of course I forgive you. Come—look at me—that's it. I don't look angry, do I?"

"N-no," admitted Beccel, with a sob. "But you must be because I was going to kill you."

"Ah! but you didn't," said Guthlac. "You changed your mind, didn't you? Now, get up and finish shaving me quickly."

"But supposing I get that awful temptation again?" asked Beccel anxiously.

"Nonsense, that's all over," said Guthlac, briskly. "If it should come back, you just fight it like anything, and I'll help you. Now come along, I can't go about half smooth and half bristly all day because of your temptations!"

But there were no more temptations for Beccel because he just did not want to kill Guthlac any more. From that time he loved him better than anyone in the world, and when Guthlac was taken with his last illness, it was Beccel who helped and comforted him until he died.

Guthlac's Friends

NOW everything was peace and quietness on the island in the Fens. The Ancient Britons had vanished; Beccel, instead of being a jealous enemy, had become a faithful friend. Even the wild beasts, birds and fishes were tame and friendly. In fact, they were so friendly that they were almost a nuisance sometimes, especially two greedy ravens who loved to fly in and out of Guthlac's home, for they would keep stealing things. However, Guthlac was very patient with them all because he loved them. He fed them every day and they obeyed him as if they had been his children.

Some of the people who came to visit the hermitage could hardly believe it when they saw how tame the birds were. Once, as Guthlac sat talking to an old friend named Wilfrith who had come to see him, two swallows came and simply perched all over him. On his head, his arms, his knees, his shoulders——

"Just look at those birds!" exclaimed Wilfrith. "Whatever makes them so tame?"

Guthlac took one of the swallows in his hand and held it against his cheek. "Why, don't you know——" he began.

"Sweet-sweet!" twittered the other swallow, indignantly. "What about me?"

"Don't you know," Guthlac began again, taking the second swallow in his other hand, "that those who live as God wishes us to will always find the birds and beasts friendly? If we stop hurting them, or fearing that they

will hurt us, what is there to prevent us being friends ? "
He opened his hands, letting the swallows fly. " It's the
same with the angels," he continued. " How can they
possibly talk to you if you will keep rushing about and
making a noise. But go away alone and just *keep quiet*,
and then you will see ! Then, maybe, they *will* come
and talk."

Swallows are all very well, but those ravens, they really
were rather a nuisance sometimes. Twice they stole things
from visitors.

Once, Guthlac had a man staying with him for a few
days, and while he was there this man remembered he had
a rather important note to write. He sat down, wrote it,
and then went off for a walk, leaving the note on the table.
When he came back it was gone ! Guthlac, coming in
from church, found his visitor just standing and staring
at the table as if he would look right through it.

" Whatever's the matter ? " he asked.

" I left a note," exclaimed the visitor, " here, on the
table—and now it's gone." He began to hunt wildly
about the room. " It can't have blown away——"

" I'm afraid," said Guthlac, " that the ravens must have
taken it. I can't get them to understand that they must
leave my guests' belongings alone."

The visitor was most annoyed.

" A nice state of affairs," he complained, " when you
can't leave anything about for fear of having it stolen by a
bird. That letter took me hours to write, and now I
suppose I shall have to begin it all over again ! "

" I shouldn't do that yet," said Guthlac. " You'll get
your letter back, don't worry. The ravens will presently
fly up through the fens. You follow in the boat—and
you'll find the note—you see if you don't."

Later that afternoon Guthlac was sitting alone when his
visitor came bursting in upon him waving something
excitedly.

" I've got it ! " he cried. " I did as you said. I took
the boat and rowed up the stream the way the ravens went

until I came to a kind of lake with a great clump of reeds in the middle. And there was my note—stuck on one of the reeds, just as if the birds had left it there on purpose!"

Another time the ravens had a game with a pair of gloves. Guthlac's friend Wilfrith brought a most important person called Athelbald to see him. After they had been talking together for some time, Guthlac said suddenly :

"By the way, did either of you leave anything in the boat ?"

"Only my gloves," said Wilfrith.

"Oh! they'll be all right," said Athelbald, who was enjoying himself and did not want to be interrupted.

Guthlac said nothing, but he wondered a little anxiously where the ravens were.

When, later on, they came out to have a look round the island, the first thing they saw was a raven, sitting on the roof with a glove in its beak.

"I say! It's got one of my gloves!" cried Wilfrith.

"Oh! dear. Oh! dear!" sighed Guthlac, shaking his head at the raven. "What shall I do with you? Don't you know it's a sin to steal—especially from a visitor ?"

By this time the raven was looking thoroughly ashamed of himself.

"Well?" said Guthlac, more sternly. "What are you going to do about it ?"

With a dismal croak, the bird flew off, leaving the glove lying on the roof top.

"Hurrah!" cried Wilfrith. He seized a long stick. "I think I can reach it with this," he said.

With the aid of the stick they managed to rescue the glove. "I'd better get the other from the boat at once," said Wilfrith.

But it was not there. "That wretched bird must have taken them both!" he exclaimed. "What a nuisance! I do think these birds should be made to behave properly. One glove is worse than useless!"

" I'm very sorry," said Guthlac meekly.   " Perhaps it will turn up presently."

A little later, as they sat talking, they heard the bell which was used as a signal by anyone who came seeking Guthlac.

" I'll go," said Guthlac.   " I won't be long."

A few moments afterwards he re-entered the room and laid something on the table in front of Wilfrith.

" Here's your other glove," said he.

" Wherever did you find it ? " asked Wilfrith, staring at it.

" Some men have just brought it," Guthlac answered. " I went down to the landing stage and there was a boat with three men in it and one of them had the glove.   They told me that they were rowing across the lake when a raven flew over their heads and dropped it in."

" Well ! " was all Wilfrith could say.

I must tell you of just one more visitor who came to Croyland, because his visit was rather important to Guthlac.

It was a Bishop named Hedda.   What with his servants, attendants and so on, there was quite a large party, and among them was a very learned man named Wigfrith. As they rode along they talked about the famous hermit they were going to see.

" I hear he's perfectly marvellous," said one of the party.   " He knows *exactly* what you are thinking the moment he sees you, and as for prophecy——"

" He certainly seems to possess strange powers," agreed the Bishop.

" Ah ! but," put in another, " where do they come from ?   That's the point.   You can't be too careful, you know.   His powers may come from the devil."

" Or he may be just a fraud," put in another.

" As to that," remarked Wigfrith, the learned one, in a rather superior tone, " I don't fancy this Guthlac will deceive *me*.   When I was living in Scotland, I met dozens of hermits and holy men.   I shall be able to tell at once if this man is a holy hermit, or merely an impostor."

"In that case," said the Bishop, dryly, "we have nothing to worry about."

Well, in due course they arrived at Guthlac's island and were soon having a good talk. At least, the Bishop and Guthlac were talking. Wigfrith, who had come specially to see him, just sat and looked superior.

The Bishop was so struck with Guthlac that suddenly, in the middle of the conversation, he said :

" Brother Guthlac, I feel that you should be a priest. Will you allow me to make you one, while I am here ? "

Guthlac gladly agreed to the Bishop's suggestion. A special service was held in the little church which Guthlac had built, and there he was ordained priest by Bishop Hedda.

Afterwards, they all sat down to a meal together, and although he did not usually eat meat, Guthlac ate it then because it was a special occasion. As soon as they had all taken their seats, Guthlac leaned across the table to Wigfrith and said, with a twinkle in his eye :

" Well, what kind of a man does the new priest seem to you ? You know, the one of whom you said that you could tell at once whether he was good or bad ? "

Wigfrith, looking awfully ashamed of himself, stammered out something.

" That's all right," laughed Guthlac, " forget it ! " After which they were all the best of friends.

The end of Guthlac's life came rather unexpectedly. He had been about fifteen years living in the Fens when one day he was taken ill in church.

Beccel was there. He rushed to help him.

" What is it ? What is the matter ? " he implored.

" Don't worry," replied Guthlac gently. " This means that I am going to die soon, that's all."

Beccel burst into tears.

" Come, come, you mustn't upset yourself," said Guthlac. " *I'm* glad."

Guthlac was ill for seven days. Easter came during that time and he insisted upon holding the Easter service himself.   But on the eighth day he was so terribly ill that he had to give up.   He died that day, and he was buried in his own little church at Croyland.

After Guthlac's death a larger church was built on the island and a group of monks settled there.   Then they built a great wooden abbey—the abbey of Croyland. The land there was good and soon the abbey was surrounded with such cornfields, orchards and vineyards, that when a famine came the monks of Croyland were able to feed all the people of the fens.

And because of the goodness of Guthlac, and the miracles that were said to happen there after his death, the place was made a Sanctuary.   That is to say, anyone who was in danger from enemies could go there for protection, and neither lords, sheriffs, nor even kings could touch them.   So long as they lived in peace with each other and worked for their living like honest men, they were safe.

The wooden abbey stood a long while, but in the end it was replaced by a stone one, and while it was being built some French monks came and opened a school in the little Roman town of Grant-brigge near by.   That town became Cambridge, and it is said that the little school was the beginning of Cambridge University.

So what with one thing and another, it seems that Saint Guthlac *was* a Man of Future Glory after all.

VIII

SAINT FRIDESWIDE—THE FAIR FUGITIVE

FRIDESWIDE is the Patron Saint of Oxford. If you go into the Cathedral there you can see her shrine, and above it, like an open picture book, a stained glass window, telling in pictures the story of her life.

This is the legend of Saint Frideswide :

Somewhere near Oxford there once lived a prince named Didan, with his wife Safrida, and they had one fair daughter.

Her name was Frideswide, and she was born about the year 650. As she grew up it was clear that Frideswide was not like most girls. They loved to dance and sing : she loved to study with her governess Alviga. They loved to chatter of the beautiful clothes they had and the handsome young men who came to woo them : she was not a bit interested in beautiful clothes or handsome young men. They dreamed of their bridal robes, but Frideswide dreamed of a nun's habit.

And so one day she came to her father, and said :

" Father dear, there is something I want very much."

" Then you shall have it, my love," responded her father, fondly.

" Thank you," said Frideswide, kissing him. " Then, please, could you build me a nunnery ? "

" A nunnery ? " exclaimed her father, greatly surprised.

" You see, Father," continued Frideswide gravely, " I mean to be a nun."

A young man stepped from the shadow of a tree.

At this, her mother, who had been sitting quietly in a corner with her work, looked up.

"That is quite impossible, my child," she said. "Your father wouldn't dream of letting you."

"Yes, I would," contradicted Didan. "I don't see why she shouldn't be a nun if she wants to."

"Then I do," said Safrida, biting off her thread with a snap. "Our only daughter a nun—I never heard of such a thing! She will marry, of course. A prince, or a king. I have thought of several who would be most suitable."

"But I don't want to marry anyone," protested Frideswide.

"Don't be silly, dear," replied her mother. "Of course you do. You will marry a noble youth of high degree. Handsome, if possible."

"But you don't understand, Mother," said Frideswide patiently. "I want to serve God, and to help all the poor and sick and unhappy people I can. That is why I must be a nun."

Safrida rose. "That will do, Frideswide," she said. She rolled up her work into a tight bundle, as though she were rolling up the argument, fastening it with a hard knot, like a determined "No." "That will do," she repeated, and sailed out of the room.

Prince Didan sighed—then smiled. "It's all right, my dear," said he, "she'll come round to it." He reached over and patted his daughter's hand. "Nuns are good women," said he, "and pleasing to God, and if you want to be one, no one shall prevent you."

The end of it was that Prince Didan built a nunnery for his daughter at Oxford and there she lived, with twelve other maidens, nursing the sick, feeding the hungry, caring for widows and orphans and those in trouble, and serving God in all her ways.

Then something happened to spoil it all.

There came one day to Prince Didan's castle a man, handsome and haughty, dressed in his very best clothes, riding his very finest horse, and surrounded by a crowd of pages, grooms and attendants.

"Prince Algar to wait upon Prince Didan!" announced his page. The castle gates were flung open. "Prince Algar to wait upon Prince Didan!" "Prince Algar to wait upon Prince Didan!" Through courtyard and corridor it echoed, to the room where Prince Didan sat.

"Bother!" said the Prince. "What does he want? Oh! all right—show him in."

Next moment Prince Algar swaggered into the room.

"Good morning," said he, bowing, but only just. "I called to ask for the hand of your daughter Frideswide. I have decided to marry her."

Prince Didan looked up. There was a gleam of triumph in his eye, but his speech was smooth as butter.

"There now," said he, "I am sorry you should have come all this way for nothing. Haven't you heard? My daughter has become a nun."

Prince Algar looked annoyed, but not very, because he was so used to having his own way that it did not occur to him that this meant that he would have to give up all idea of marrying Frideswide.

"That's all right," said he. "A beautiful girl like the Lady Frideswide certainly won't need to spend her life in a nunnery. Just send for her, will you? When she hears that *I* am willing to marry her——"

"I'm afraid you don't understand," interrupted Prince Didan quietly. "My daughter has chosen to give her life to God and His service. There is no question of her marrying anyone."

Still Prince Algar was quite confident. "Nonsense," said he, "young girls often get these fancies, but they wear off. Once she hears about me, she'll soon change her mind."

"You don't know my daughter if you imagine that," replied Prince Didan. "It is no use, Prince, what you want is impossible."

Then the Prince lost his temper.

" Impossible, is it ? " he shouted. " We'll soon see about that ! Let me tell you, what I want is *never* impossible ! "

With that, he flounced out of the castle and galloped off to find the nunnery where Frideswide lived, for he was quite determined to marry her. He soon found the place, and from that time poor Frideswide did not have a moment's peace. Prince Algar simply haunted her. In vain did she send word to tell him she could not and would not marry him. He hung about outside the nunnery, lying in wait for her. If she walked in the garden, he looked over the wall. If she went to the chapel, he peered through the window. If she went to visit the sick, he followed her, begging and imploring her to leave her nunnery and come and marry him. The more firmly she refused him, the more determined was he to marry her.

At last, when he found that she really would not be persuaded, he decided to carry her off by force.

He collected some of his men, and one dark night they gathered outside the nunnery walls. The nuns, sleeping peacefully in their cells, were wakened by strange noises. One climbed upon her bed and peeped from her window.

" Prince Algar ! " she shrieked. With cries of terror the nuns all rushed into the corridor. " What shall we do ? " " Whatever shall we do ? " they asked each other.

Suddenly, Frideswide stood in her doorway.

" Hush ! " she said gently. " You are in no danger. The Prince means no harm to anyone but me. Go quietly to the chapel and stay there till morning. If the Prince tries to force his way in, do not stop him. Let him go where he will. When he finds I am not here, he will leave you in peace."

" But you, Sister Frideswide ? " asked one nun timidly. " What about you ? "

" I must leave here at once," Frideswide answered. " I shall seek a hiding place down the river. Two of you come with me to bring back the boat——" Her voice was drowned suddenly by a shower of blows on the door. " Quickly," she cried, " to the chapel.   Good-bye, sisters, and pray for me."   Then, beckoning two of her favourite nuns to go with her, she sped swiftly down the corridor that led to the garden.

The nunnery garden sloped to the river bank. Moored beside it was a little boat.   Silently, Frideswide and her companions climbed in and loosed it from its moorings.

" I will steer," said Frideswide.   " Sister Aletha, can you manage the oars ? "

" I—I think so," panted Sister Aletha, struggling with them.   " It's just that they're—rather *large*."

The boat rocked wildly.   " Oh, dear ! Oh, dear ! " wailed the other nun.   " We shall all be drowned, I know we shall."

Suddenly, a young man stepped from the shadow of a tree on the bank.   At least, it seemed so, though they all agreed afterwards that they had not noticed him before, which was strange, seeing that he was dressed in white. He came forward silently, his feet made no sound, and— was it the newly risen moon that made a light about his head ?

Without speaking, the young man stepped into the boat, took the oars gently from Sister Aletha, and began to row with long, steady strokes.

The two nuns looked at each other.   " Is it an angel ? " whispered Sister Aletha.   " I—I think so," her companion whispered back. Frideswide said nothing.   The young man only smiled.

At last they came to Abingdon.

" Here," said Frideswide, and steered for the bank. The young man shipped his oars, jumped ashore and held the boat for Frideswide to land.   Then, lifting his hand in a gesture half blessing, half farewell, he vanished.

" It *was* an angel," breathed Sister Aletha, in awestruck tones.

Frideswide gathered up the little bundle of belongings she had brought with her, and turned to go.

"Good-bye, dear sisters," she said. "Be careful how you row back. Tell the others not to worry—I shall be quite safe. Good-bye, and God bless you." She stood a moment watching them start upon their homeward journey, then turned towards the wooded shores where she hoped to find safe hiding.

She found it at last, deep hidden in the woods. A little hut—a place once used to keep pigs in.

"Well, I never expected to live in a pigsty," she laughed as she crawled inside. "But anything is better than having that awful Prince Algar worrying me." She settled down in this strange cell and there she lived for three years.

.   .   .   .   .

But even there she was not safe from Prince Algar. Having made sure she was not in the nunnery, he went off in a fury, determined to search the countryside until he found her, and at last, just as Frideswide was beginning to think that she really had shaken him off, he discovered her secret hiding-place in the woods.

Then began a kind of terrible game of hide-and-seek between them. Frideswide had constantly to be on the watch. The moment she caught sight of Algar coming towards her cell she would slip away and hide in the woods. There she would lie while he searched—all the time in dread of discovery—until he gave it up and went away. Then she would creep back, with a sigh of thankfulness, to her cell. But presently, back would come Prince Algar once more, and the game of hide-and-seek would begin all over again. The longer it went on, the more determined Algar became and the more weary Frideswide. She would have gone to her father for help, but Prince Algar was more powerful than he, and she feared to bring his vengeance upon her parents if they had anything to do with the matter.

At last, when she was so tired that she began to think she could struggle no longer, she remembered two good saints who had always been her friends—Saint Catherine and Saint Cecilia.

" Oh ! sweet Saint Catherine, good Saint Cecilia," she prayed, " do, please, help me. I am so *tired*. Do, do make Prince Algar leave me in peace."

" But certainly we will, my dear," replied the Saints. " Why ever didn't you ask us before ? "

Now, at that moment, Prince Algar was riding furiously to Oxford, for he had made up his mind to have another good try to catch Frideswide. But Saint Catherine and Saint Cecilia had not promised their help for nothing. As the prince reached the gates of Oxford, he was struck blind.

With a great cry, he checked his horse. His servants ran to him, asking what was the matter.

" Something has happened to my eyes," answered the Prince, in a dazed tone. " Lead me home. I—*I can't see*."

They led him home, and set him in his great chair by the hearth—stone blind.

" Leave me alone," he said. " Go—all of you—about your business. Go ! "

" And—and the Lady Frideswide ? " ventured his page, timidly.

" The Lady Frideswide has won," answered Prince Algar.

" It's all right, my dear," said the two Saints to Frideswide. " You can go back to Oxford quite safely. Prince Algar won't trouble you any more. He is blind."

Feeling tremendously relieved, Frideswide set off for Oxford. She was walking along, thinking how nice it would be to be home again, and how pleased the other nuns would be to see her, when she saw, coming towards her, a most pitiful sight. A young man who was a leper.

When he saw who she was (for by this time Frideswide was known all over the district) the leper stopped and said humbly : " I beseech the Virgin Frideswide, by the Almighty God, to kiss me in the name of His Only Son."

Frideswide stood quite still. To kiss a leper ! The mere thought filled her with horror. Then came another feeling—pity. And pity drove out horror, like sunshine driving away darkness. Making the sign of the Cross, she bent and kissed the young leper on the lips, and from that moment he was cured.

Frideswide had a wonderful welcome from the nuns when she arrived, and when they heard that Prince Algar had ceased to pursue her, they were delighted.

" It was Saint Catherine and Saint Cecilia who helped me," she told them. " Wasn't it kind of them ? Only I —I do rather wish they hadn't had to make him blind. It must be so awful to be blind."

" He deserved it," said Sister Aletha, sternly. " He was a great sinner."

" Yes, I know," agreed Frideswide, sighing. " But, all the same——"

She could not get Prince Algar out of her mind. It was lovely not to have him worrying her any more, but— it must be so terrible to be blind ! At last she just could not bear it. " Sweet Saint Catherine, Good Saint Cecilia," she prayed. " If Prince Algar promises *faithfully* to leave me alone, couldn't you give him back his sight ? "

" Why, certainly, my dear, if you wish it," replied the Saints. And Prince Algar, sitting alone in darkness, suddenly saw again the glory of light.

But because of his fate, the kings of England fancied there must be something dangerous to kings at Oxford, and not until the reign of Henry II would they dare to enter the city, for fear they, too, might be struck blind.

From that time, Frideswide lived quite happily at her nunnery, nursing the sick, feeding the hungry, caring for widows and orphans and those in trouble, and serving God in all her ways. She built a chapel in the wood at Thornbury, and at Binsey, a little village near Oxford, there is a spring which is said to have come forth in answer

H

to her prayers.   As for her nunnery—that became Christ Church College, Oxford, and her little chapel was rebuilt and is now the Cathedral.

When Frideswide was dying, she saw in a vision her friends Saint Catherine and Saint Cecilia.

"It's quite all right, my dear," they told her. "We shall be here to meet you when you come."

IX

SAINT DUNSTAN—COUNSELLOR
OF KINGS

Little and Good

"HE'S terribly small," said the mother, looking down at her newly born son as he lay in her arms.

"Don't you worry about that, my dear," said her husband. "Don't you worry about that a bit. Good things are done up in small parcels, you know!"

"And good he is, the treasure," put in the nurse, giving the baby a smacking kiss. "Little and good—that's what he is—bless him!"

The place where the baby was born was near Glastonbury in Somerset: the time was the year 925, and the name of the baby was Dunstan. His father was a nobleman, and it is even said that there was royal blood in the baby's veins, but royal or no, he certainly was not what you would call a bonny baby.

As he grew older his mother often looked at him and sighed. He was so very small and frail looking.

"Don't you fret, Madam," the nurse repeated. "I shouldn't wonder if he were to shoot up like one o'clock one of these days, and surprise us all."

"Brains," said his father, "that's what it is—brains. Our Dunstan's a brainy one and you can't expect to have brains *and* brawn. But never you mind—brains will beat brawn any day."

He never did shoot up as the nurse promised, but his

Dunstan warned King Ethelred that his reign would be full of trouble.

father was certainly right about the brains. It soon became clear that Dunstan was a very clever boy indeed. Not only was he brilliant at his lessons, but he could draw and paint, make wood carvings, do fine metal work, and play most beautifully on the harp. As for his handwriting, it was clearer and finer than the finest print. Of course there was no print in those days. Every copy of every book had to be written by hand, so that writing itself was quite an art. You can see, in some of our museums, some of the books which Dunstan made. Lovely books, written in his fine, clear writing, with little, brightly coloured scenes from the Bible as illustrations, or pictures of birds and animals twined about the capital letters. *Illuminating*, it is called, and a very good name too, for even to-day the colours are so bright that they really do seem to light up the page.

Dunstan went to school at Glastonbury Abbey. Some of the cleverest scholars of the time lived there. You could get the best education in England at Glastonbury. Dunstan was soon top boy, but he was not a bit proud or domineering. In fact, he was a rather quiet, dreamy sort of boy, always going off into daydreams, or declaring that he had had a vision. The other boys laughed, and teased him a little, but secretly they were rather proud of him.

When he had been at Glastonbury a little while, he was taken seriously ill with a kind of brain fever. He was delirious, and made such a noise that he kept the other boys awake at night with his raving.

" This won't do at all," said the teachers. " We can't have the whole school disturbed like this. We had better get some country woman to nurse him."

By the time they had found one, Dunstan was so ill that no one thought he would live.

" It's all this studying," declared a big boy, who was certainly more brawn than brain. " My father says it isn't healthy. He says you shouldn't *worry* your brains, and I quite agree with him."

"Is that why you are always bottom of the class?" asked a little boy, cheekily.

"I think it's quite *safe* to study," remarked a serious looking boy, "so long as you don't overdo it."

They argued the matter for awhile. Then, being very full of their own affairs, they forgot all about Dunstan and his illness.

They soon had a reminder, however. One night the whole place was upset—Dunstan was lost!

"The very first time I've left him!" wailed the woman, who had been nursing him. "Sat by his bed, I have, night after night, until my husband, he says to me—'Wife, this won't do. Sleep you must, or you'll be ill yourself. Leave the lad, and go and lie down awhile. If he starts his raving we shall soon hear him.' 'I'll just put my head on the pillow for five minutes,' I said—and so I did. And, would you believe it, when I went again to look at him he'd vanished!"

A groan came from the group of neighbours who had been listening to the story with much relish.

"He's drowned—that's what's happened to him," remarked a stout woman, gloomily.

"Carried off by the devil, more likely," added another.

Meanwhile the search was going on. Suddenly one of Dunstan's school-mates came running to the monks who were seeking him.

"I've found him! I've found him!" he shouted. "He's on the church tower!"

"Nonsense," said one of the monks. "The church door is locked. He could not possibly get up there."

"Yes he could, Father," answered the boy. "The ladder is still there. You know, the one the men used when they were mending the roof——"

"Let us go and see," said the monk.

But when they reached the church there was no sign of Dunstan.

"But I saw him," persisted the boy. "He was walking along, right at the very edge and——" he lowered his voice "—*there was someone with him, guiding him.*"

"You're making it up," said the boy who didn't believe in study.

It was not until morning that Dunstan was found, and then it was not *on*, but *in* the church. The first monks to enter the church discovered him lying on the floor, half dressed and sound asleep.

He was carried quickly back to bed again.

" Poor lamb ! " cried the woman, who had been nursing him, " I fear he'll have taken his death of cold."

But no—not only did Dunstan take no harm from his adventure, but when he woke from his sleep the fever was gone, and he was soon quite well.

" But how did you get into the church ? " demanded his schoolfellows, when he rejoined them.

" You walked on the roof, didn't you, Dunstan ? " said the boy who had claimed to have seen him there.

Dunstan hesitated, frowning a little.

" Well," he began slowly, " it was like this. I—I woke up—at least, I *thought* I woke up—and felt quite well. So I thought I'd go to church to thank God for it. There wasn't anybody with me, so I got up and dressed and went to the church—only on the way everything got all muddled again—I suppose it was the fever really. I remember thinking some wild dogs were chasing me—and trying to beat them off—and then running to the church and finding the door locked. And I remember going up the ladder on to the roof, and walking on the parapet—and—and that's all."

" You must have gone down the belfry stairs into the church," suggested one boy. " It's a wonder you weren't killed."

" I think there was an angel looking after me," replied Dunstan, dreamily.

" I can't see," remarked the boy, who didn't believe in study, as the group broke up, " why Dunstan should have angels looking after him, any more than anyone else."

Dunstan did not stay much longer at Glastonbury, for he was called to the Court of King Athelstane. It was the custom for youths of noble blood to spend some time attending on the King, and he found several of his relatives already there as pages.

He had a good start, for the King took a great fancy to him. " That boy," he told everyone, " is something quite out of the common. You should hear him on the harp ! And as for sound sense and good judgment—why ! he's a regular Solomon, young as he is."

Often the King would call for Dunstan to come and play his harp, and sing to him. Or, if he had to decide some quarrel between two of his subjects, the boy would be sent for.

" Come along, my young Solomon," the King would cry. " Come and see what you can make of this." And what Dunstan made of it was always fair and just and often much wiser than many of his elders would have done.

The ladies of the Court were fond of Dunstan, too. Because he was gentle and delicate looking they loved to make much of him. Sometimes he would play and sing to them : sometimes sketch designs for their embroidery.

Carrying his harp, he came one morning to a room where some of the Court ladies were gathered at their work. Presently, one of them begged him to draw her a design for a stole which she wanted to embroider.

Dunstan was only too pleased. He hung up his harp on a nail by the window and set to work. The ladies gathered round to watch him, and they were all intent on the design, when suddenly there floated through the air a sweet, soft strain of music.

They all looked at each other in astonishment.

" It's in this room ! " gasped one lady.

" But no one is playing ! " whispered another.

All at once, one of the ladies sprang up, her face pale with fright. She pointed with shaking finger to where Dunstan's harp hung.

" It's coming from the harp ! " she screamed. " The harp is playing by itself ! "

Instantly, the whole party of ladies rushed to the door.

" Witchcraft ! sorcery ! " they shrieked. " The harp is playing by magic ! " Pushing and jostling each other in their anxiety to get away, they tumbled somehow out of the room. In a few minutes Dunstan found himself alone.

You really cannot blame those ladies. They lived in a time of great ignorance, when everything that was not understood was put down to witchcraft or something of that kind. But Dunstan had the kind of mind that does not take fright at everything new and strange, but instead, asks " Why ? " and " How ? "

The harp was still playing softly to itself. He went nearer to it—listened intently—moved it a little—listened again—tried it in a new place——

" The wind ? " he said to himself at last. " Yes, it must be. The wind, blowing through the harpstrings. But that's interesting. That's an *idea !* "

And so it was—the idea of the Aeolian Harp.

The affair of the harp caused quite a lot of talk at Court. The ladies were only too pleased to tell their tale, and like most tales, it grew in the telling. There were plenty to listen, too. A harp that played of itself ! That was something like a story ! " Witchcraft," said some. " Black magic, that's what it is. Dunstan is a dangerous fellow." Others said : " Angels' voices. Dunstan is one of God's favoured ones ; the angels sing and play for him."

Nobody took the least notice of Dunstan's explanation about the wind on the harp strings.

Now, when anyone is particularly popular and successful, there is often someone else who is jealous. In Dunstan's case it was his fellow-pages (some of them his own relations) who were the jealous ones. It did not seem to strike them that he was more successful than they because he worked harder, or better liked for the simple reason that he was much nicer. Oh ! no. " *Favouritism,*" they said. "*Black Magic*," they said. The more fuss the King made of Dunstan, the more they hated him, until nothing would do but they must be rid of him altogether. They began to whisper more and more spiteful things about him. They mocked him when he spoke of his dreams and visions and jeered at him for spending so much time at his prayers.

They seized at once on the story of the harp. "There you are, you see!" they exclaimed. "Black Magic!" So the whispers grew and the jealousy grew, until at last one of the pages dared to accuse Dunstan of sorcery before the King.

"What? What?" cried His Majesty. "My little Solomon a sorcerer—I'll not believe it."

"It is true, Your Majesty," said one of the pages. "You don't know half what goes on. He sees things that no one else sees. He talks when there is no one to talk to——"

"There was that business of the harp, Your Majesty," put in another page.

"That was strange, certainly," admitted the King. "But Dunstan said it was the wind."

"The wind!" scoffed the first page. "Do other harps play without a harper? It was the work of the devil!"

"Then the devil must have a very good ear for music," said the King, tartly, "for I hear the tune was wonderfully sweet." "Some say," he added, "that it was the hands of angels that plucked the harp strings."

But Dunstan's enemies were determined. Somehow they would get rid of this small, dreamy boy, who was always putting them in the shade. They continued their whispering and hinting until even the King began to doubt, and at last Dunstan was expelled from the Court.

Dazed and unhappy, scarcely knowing how or why it had happened, he trudged along the road, neither knowing nor caring which way he took, so long as he got away from those who had accused him so unjustly. But they had not finished with him yet. Suddenly, out from the woods on

either side of the road sprang a yelling, jeering crowd—
those very same pages whose jealousy had been the cause
of all his trouble.

"Here he is!" they shouted to each other. "Here's the
dreamer! Here's the harp player—here's the King's Good
Boy. Now we've got him just where we want him!"

"Let me pass, please," said Dunstan, trying to get
by them.

But they spread out all across the road.

"Not so fast," said the eldest page. "We've got a
little business with you yet. Come on, boys!"

Beside the road was a pond thick with mud and slime.
The boys seized Dunstan and flung him into it. For a
few moments they stood laughing and jeering at him, and
some even pushed him further into the mud with their feet.
Then they left him and rushed off, roaring with laughter.

Luckily the pond was not deep enough to drown in.
Somehow he managed to struggle out. As he scrambled
up the bank, soaking wet and covered with mud, he heard
the barking of dogs. The boys had let loose upon him
some fierce hounds kept by the King.

But there they made a mistake. Dunstan loved animals,
and they loved him. The hounds, bounding forward to
tear an enemy to pieces, found a friend instead. In a
moment they were leaping about him, licking his hands
and face and almost knocking him over with their clumsy
embraces, while Dunstan, hugging them, felt that sometimes dogs could be kinder than men.

At last he wiped his face and clothes as well as he could,
and, telling the dogs to go home, continued his journey.
He had decided to make for Winchester, where a relation
of his, named Elphege, was the Bishop.

Bishop Elphege was astonished when the wet, weary
and bedraggled little figure appeared.

"Why, Dunstan, my boy," he exclaimed, "what has
happened?"

"I have been expelled from Court," answered Dunstan,
sitting down wearily.

"But how did you get into that plight?" asked the Bishop. Then, seeing how tired Dunstan looked, he added quickly: "Never mind about that now. You want a meal and a rest and some dry clothes. You can tell me all about it afterwards."

"Well, you had better stay with me for the present," said the Bishop, when he had heard Dunstan's story. "Don't worry about losing your place at Court. You were meant for something better than a courtier. I believe God has other work for you."

"I shall do whatever He wishes, of course," answered Dunstan.

Yet, when the Bishop suggested what that might be, he hesitated. For the Bishop thought he should be a monk—giving up his whole life to God's service, and at first Dunstan did not like the idea of it.

"But I can serve God and still live like other people," he argued. "Surely He does not want us all to be monks and priests?"

"Of course not," answered the Bishop, "but I believe He wants *you* to be one. Think it over and listen to what *He* says to you."

But before he could make up his mind, Dunstan fell ill again. While he was ill he had a great deal of time for thinking, and in the end he came to the conclusion that his uncle was right.

When he was well again he came to the Bishop and said:

"I have decided. I mean to enter the Church. If that is what God wants me to do, I want it too."

Abbot of Glastonbury

HAVING made up his mind, Dunstan wasted no time, but returned to Glastonbury to begin his new life there.

The first thing he did when he got there was to build himself a cell to live in. It was 5 feet by $2\frac{1}{2}$ feet (just measure that out, and see how you would like to live in a house that size). Dunstan not only lived there, studying, praying, copying books and putting in all those bright pictures, but he also found time (and space) for his metal work, making bells and sacred vessels for the Church.

There's a quaint legend of how the devil came to tempt him there, disguised as a beautiful lady. He was working at his forge at the time, and, having an idea that there was a trick somewhere, he snatched up a pair of red-hot tongs, and nipped his visitor's nose ! Thereupon, the devil gave such a yell as no lady could or would have uttered, and so betrayed himself.

When Dunstan had been at Glastonbury some time, King Athelstane died and was succeeded by his brother Edmund. No sooner was the new King settled on his throne than he sent for Dunstan to come back to Court.

What a triumph ! He who had been sent away in disgrace, thrown into a pond and set upon by dogs, now came back in honour to be the new King's adviser !

Unfortunately it did not last long. It was the same old story. Though the King was his friend, there were others who were his enemies. They envied him the King's favour : they were jealous of his power and influence in the country. The foolish ones resented his wisdom : the bad ones hated his goodness. Soon they began to plot how to get rid of him. They told the King lies about him, and the King was stupid enough to believe them. For the second time, Dunstan was sent away from the Court in disgrace.

He went quietly back to Glastonbury. Back to his tiny cell : to his writing and painting : his music and metal work.

But King Edmund did not feel comfortable. The things those jealous men had told him about Dunstan had seemed perfectly true at the time. But now—he wondered. When he thought of Dunstan's face and voice, he felt dreadfully worried. Because they did not seem to fit the things the others had said about him. Supposing he had been mistaken ? He thought about it often, especially at night when he was just going to sleep.

At last one night the King simply could not sleep for thinking about Dunstan. He got up feeling very bad tempered. " I'll go hunting," said he. " That will take my mind off—off *everything*."

So away he went with just a few attendants. Presently they started a deer, and the King, in the excitement of the chase, forgot his worries. He was galloping gloriously along when all at once he saw that some of his dogs had checked. The deer had come to the edge of a deep ravine, and, fear giving it strength, had leapt clean across to the cliff on the other side. Some of the dogs managed to leap after it, but the rest stood trembling and yelping on the brink. Meanwhile, the King's horse was galloping madly towards the spot where the deer had leapt. Frantically, the King tugged at the reins, but the horse had taken fright and would not stop. " It's too wide—he'll never do it," the King thought wildly. " We shall both go over the precipice ! We shall be killed ! "

He could hear his attendants galloping after him, but their horses were not so good as his—they would never catch up with him in time !

And suddenly, he thought of Dunstan. He seemed to see his face—to hear his voice—and as the horse dashed nearer and nearer to the ravine, he prayed frantically : " Let the horse stop ! Please, God, let the horse stop, and I'll make it up to Dunstan ! "

The horse did stop—only just in time. Both horse and rider were trembling. Then the King's attendants galloped up to him.

" Your Majesty is safe ? " " Your Majesty is unhurt ? " they asked anxiously.

" I'm quite all right," said the King. " But we'll go home. I've done with hunting for to-day. There is something else I have to do."

As soon as he arrived home the King sent for one of his most trusted men. " Fetch Dunstan," he commanded.

Wondering a little, Dunstan came into the presence of the King.

" Quickly," said His Majesty, " have your horse saddled. I want you to ride with me."

Wondering still more, Dunstan obeyed. The King led the way towards Glastonbury. As soon as they arrived he made for the church, Dunstan still following. For a little while they knelt and prayed together. Then the King stood up, took the still mystified Dunstan by the hand, led him to the Abbot's chair and put him into it, saying solemnly :

" You are to be the possessor and defender of this throne, and if there is anything you need for the Church or the services I will pay for it out of my own treasury."

So Dunstan became Abbot of Glastonbury.

" And I'm terribly sorry I believed all those awful

things they said about you," said the King, as they left the church together. " I knew all the time, really, that they couldn't be true."

Dunstan's Work for England

ALWAYS think of Saint Dunstan as the Saint who had six kings to deal with. Not all together, of course, but he lived through the reigns of six kings. And very trying they must have been, too, some of them.

As soon as King Edmund made him Abbot of Glastonbury he began to make improvements, not only there, but in other abbeys and monasteries in England. Some of these had not kept up to the high ideals with which they had started, and Dunstan meant to try to bring them back to these high standards. So he sent away those monks who were not good enough to be serving God in His Church, and put better ones in their places. Then he went on a kind of tour to the schools and monasteries of England, explaining to them what he thought was wrong, and asking them all to try to live more like Our Lord had done.

Another of Dunstan's dreams was to make England one kingdom under one king. At that time it was divided up into small kingdoms with a different king for each, with the result that sooner or later there was war, which was bad for everyone. But Dunstan loved peace —was he not the servant of God, and Our Lord who is called the Prince of Peace ? So a great part of his life was spent in trying to make England into one peaceful kingdom, and before he died that had practically happened.

In the meantime, he thought it might help if everyone learnt as many as possible of what are called the arts of peace—that is, all those things in which you make something instead of destroying something—like music and painting and writing, beautiful needlework and all the other handicrafts. Also, he thought the people should be better educated, because that helps too. "And this," said he, "must be the work of the Church. Every monk should learn some handicraft, so that he can teach it to the people. And those that are good scholars can help to educate them. We must be the leaders and teachers of the people, so that we may keep them from paganism and war, and turn their hearts to Christianity and peace."

So Dunstan worked hard to make his dreams come true, and many other monks and priests worked with him. As for the kings, sometimes they helped, and sometimes they made things as difficult as possible.

After a short reign, King Edmund was assassinated. He left two sons, but as they were both too young to reign, his brother Edred became king.

Edred was one of the kings who helped. He gave Dunstan money to rebuild Glastonbury Abbey, and did everything he could to see that his work for England and the Church went well. During his reign Dunstan had great power. The King made him his High Treasurer, and he was his chief adviser.

Edred reigned for ten years. Then he died, and Edmund's elder son, Edwy, came to the throne.

Now everything was changed. Edwy was a most unpleasant young man—proud, domineering, selfish—with neither good heart nor good manners, as you can tell from what happened at his Coronation feast.

It was, of course, a very important occasion. All the chief men in the realm were there. Suddenly, they looked round—the King was gone! He had slipped away to another room with some special friends—the Lady Aethelgifu and her daughter Elgiva, whom he wanted to marry.

The guests were indignant. "Disgraceful," they said. "Shameful!" "Are these royal manners?"

Dunstan said nothing. He acted.

He and the Bishop of London went straight to the room in which the King and the two ladies were sitting.

"Well, what is it?" asked the King, impatiently, as they entered.

"Your Majesty," said Dunstan, "your guests await you."

"Oh! let them wait," said the King rudely.

"Your Majesty," said Dunstan gravely, "these gentlemen have come—many of them from afar—to honour you on your Coronation Day. You cannot leave them like this."

"I can do as I like," snapped Edwy. "I'm the King, aren't I? Tell them I'm busy. A lot of boring old men," he whispered to Elgiva. "I can't be bothered with them."

Dunstan's eyes flashed. "Without the support of these boring old men, Your Majesty," he said, "I doubt if you would keep your throne long." Then his tone grew sterner. "You will come back with me at once," he said, and moved towards the King.

Edwy drew back. He was furious, but he was frightened too. "Leave me alone! I'm not coming!" he cried weakly.

Dunstan simply took the King firmly by the wrist and drew him to his feet. "On the contrary," said he, "you are coming back to your guests *now*." Gripping the King's wrist tightly he led him back to the great hall. Outside the door he released him and, stepping back, allowed the King to enter the room before him.

"I'll never forgive you for this," muttered the King furiously. Then, with a very ill-grace, he re-entered the hall.

The King did not forgive Dunstan. He never had liked him. Now he hated him and was determined to be revenged upon him. There was plenty of opportunity. Dunstan had many friends, but he had many enemies too. He always did have, because he tried to make the world better, and there are always people who want it to stay exactly as it is, and can't bear anyone who wants to change it.   These were the people who were the enemies of Dunstan.   They now found a great supporter in the King.

He began by accusing Dunstan of having stolen the money given him by King Edred.

" Now then," he cried—very brave with all his courtiers around him—" What have you done with all that money ? I want to know exactly how you have spent every penny ! "

" Most of it I spent on improving Glastonbury Abbey," replied Dunstan quietly.   " That, as you know, was what it was given me for."

Edwy was beaten for the time, but this only made him all the more angry, partly because he wanted to put Dunstan in the wrong, and partly because he wanted to get hold of the money for himself.   He revenged himself by doing all he could to spoil Dunstan's work for the Church. Dunstan was heartbroken to see his work wasted, but he was helpless against the King.

At last, some of the monks who had not liked his reforms complained against him to the King.   That gave King Edwy the opportunity he was waiting for.   He banished Dunstan from England.

For the third time in his life Dunstan left the Court in disgrace, but this time he was obliged not only to leave the Court, but to leave his native country altogether.

" Sweet Father Dunstan "

DUNSTAN went to Flanders and stayed four years.   Then King Edwy died and his brother Edgar became king.

This made a great difference to Dunstan.   King Edgar called him back from Flanders and made him Bishop of Winchester.   He helped him to bring back the good monks and clergy whom Edwy had driven away.   He gave money for building more churches and to finish the work on Glastonbury Abbey.   In fact, he was just the opposite of his brother Edwy in every way.   This was the happiest time of Dunstan's life, because he was able to work for

God and England without interference, and because he and the King were real friends.

The people of England were happy during Edgar's reign, too. Like Dunstan, he hated wars and quarrels, and he was so just and kind that he made the other Kings and Princes in the country his friends, so that they gladly owned him as their chief, and instead of fighting each other, they used all to go out on the river together. Even the Danes did not invade England while Edgar ruled. No wonder he was called Edgar the Peaceable !

After a while, King Edgar made Dunstan Archbishop of Canterbury. But in spite of holding such a high position Dunstan did not forget his old friends at Glastonbury. As often as he could he visited the monks there, and the boys in the school. He knew each one and counted them all as his friends.

Nor did he forget his music. He still found time to practise the harp, and compose. One night he had a curious dream about music. It was rather like the dream that the poet Caedmon had. He dreamt he was at a wedding party. Some minstrels were singing and playing and he was listening to them, when one of the harpers— a young man, dressed in white—came to him and said, " Sir, why don't you join in the singing ? " " Because I don't know the words or the tune," replied Dunstan, in his dream. Thereupon, the young harper sat down and played and sang to him and when he woke, he found himself repeating the words and music of the harper's song. " Why ! " said he to himself, quite excited, " This is *good !* " and thereupon he called together the singers of Canterbury and taught it to them.

But Dunstan's happy time soon came to an end, for while he was still quite young his friend King Edgar died.

King Edgar had been married twice and when he died he left one son by his first wife, a boy of fourteen named Edward, and by his second wife he left a girl and another boy named Ethelred.

No sooner was their father dead than there began to

be trouble as to which of the two boys should be King. Dunstan favoured Edward, first because he was the elder son, and second, because he was fourteen, which was grown-up in those days, while Ethelred was only a little boy of about seven. But there were others who wanted Ethelred to be King, and the chief of these, as you might expect, was his mother, King Edgar's second wife, Elgiva. So there were two parties—those for Edward, headed by Dunstan, and those for Ethelred, led by his mother, Elgiva.

Now, that might very easily have meant war, so Dunstan, and some of the other Bishops, seeing how things were, took young Edward and anointed him King at once. The people were pleased, for they knew and liked Edward, but Elgiva, of course, was indignant.

In this not very happy way the new King's reign began. From the first it was rather a troubled one, because the King was so young that some of the older nobles did not like having to obey him, even though they owned him as their King. Then, when Dunstan supported him, they said he took too much upon himself. Altogether, there were a great many arguments about the government of the kingdom, and many meetings were held to try and settle them. At one of these there was a dreadful accident. The floor of the hall in which it was being held gave way, and the whole meeting fell through into the foundations beneath—except Dunstan, who, as he was chairman, was sitting in a different place. Many Lords, Knights, Bishops and Nobles were killed in that accident and the rest injured, but Dunstan was quite unhurt, and some of his friends said that God had saved him to show that he was in the right.

Now, all this time Queen Elgiva had never ceased to plot how to make her son King. People could fall through the floor—or fly up through the ceiling—for all she cared, so long as her son was crowned King. And, since she did not care what she did to get her wish, she did get it— by having King Edward murdered !

Elgiva was triumphant, but her triumph was spoiled by Ethelred himself. He was only a little boy and he had loved his big brother Edward dearly. When he learned that he was dead he just cried and cried.

" Stop that, you silly little thing ! " scolded his mother, " Stop it at once or I'll beat you. Don't you understand ? You are King now. King ! "

" I don't want to be King," wept Ethelred. " I want Edward ! "

Now the bad old times came back again. When Dunstan crowned Ethelred King he warned him that because he had come to the throne through murder his reign would be full of trouble, and he was right. One misfortune followed another, and what was worse, one invasion of Danes followed another.

It is not very surprising to find that Ethelred did not turn out very well. With such a mother, how could he ? The nice little boy who would rather have had his big brother than his big brother's crown soon gave place to a young man who was not at all the kind to make a good king. The older he grew the worse he treated Dunstan, who was by now growing an old man. Ethelred defied and insulted him, and took away much of his power, until at last Dunstan decided to take no more part in state affairs.

He went back to Canterbury and there he lived very peacefully for the last years of his life. He had always been keen on education and now he began to take a great interest in the school attached to the Cathedral. He loved to teach the boys there, and to tell them stories, which pleased the boys very much—especially the stories, as you can imagine. They all grew very fond of him and one of the boys, when he grew up, wrote Dunstan's life.

Two days before Ascension Day, in the year 988, Dunstan preached a most wonderful sermon. Those who heard him never forgot it, nor what followed, for after the sermon he wished them all good-bye, telling them that he was going on a long journey. It was not until Ascension

Day that they were sure what he meant, for on that day he died.

But his memory did not die, for long afterwards the little boys at the Cathedral School at Canterbury, when they had been naughty, used to pray for help in lightening their punishment to " Sweet Father Dunstan."

He loved to stand alone with the wind and the sea.

X

SAINT GODRIC—THE UNEXPECTED SAINT

The Seed is Sown

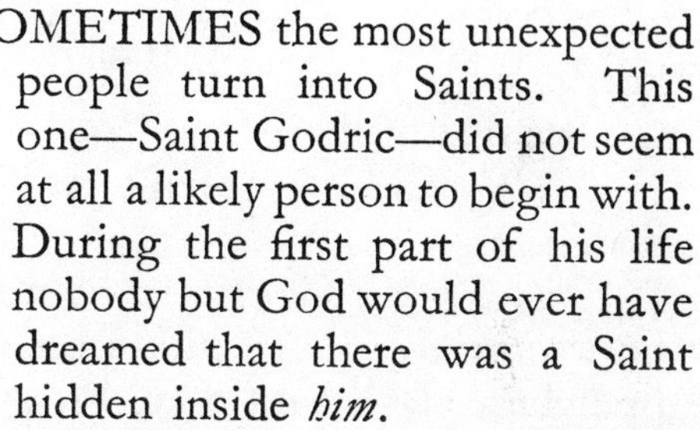

SOMETIMES the most unexpected people turn into Saints. This one—Saint Godric—did not seem at all a likely person to begin with. During the first part of his life nobody but God would ever have dreamed that there was a Saint hidden inside *him*.

Godric was born about 1065 at a place called Walpole, near the Wash. (Where King John lost all his treasure, you remember.) His parents were poor, so he had to begin quite early to earn his own living.

Most of the boys he knew worked on the land, but Godric did not fancy that at all. Instead, he decided to try his luck as a pedlar.

First, he bought a few things and sold them to people in the villages near his home. Then, with the money he got from selling these, he bought more, and tried the villages further away. Soon he was able to bring home quite a nice little stock of money to his parents.

Godric was pleased with himself. "I'm doing well," said he. "What's more, I'm going to do still better."

Sure enough, he did. He began to venture further afield, scorning the villages, and making for the towns, where there were more customers. For four years he walked the countryside with his pack, and by the time he was grown-up he had quite a nice little pedlar's business.

Suddenly, he got tired of that, and decided to go to sea.

He had seen a good deal of England and Scotland by this time. It would be fun to go to other countries, and to sail the seas. He might take some of his stock with him, too, and do a little peddling in foreign parts.

" Mother," he announced one day, " I'm going to sea."

" Are you, dear ? " said his mother. " Mind you take plenty of warm clothes then."

His father frowned a little. " What that boy will do next," he exclaimed, " there's no telling ! "

" Don't you worry," said Godric's mother. " He knows what he's about. We're going to be proud of our Godric one of these days."

" Who said we weren't proud of him now ? " growled his father.

So off went Godric to be a sailor. A fine, big fellow he was by this time, with a broad chest and arms like oak branches, black hair, wide brow, and a great hooked nose between flashing grey eyes.

And a fine sailor he made too. In fact, he became so clever at judging the weather, and such a good steersman, that whenever it seemed that a storm was coming, the Captain would send for him to take the wheel.

" Ah ! " the sailors would say, when they saw the sky beginning to darken, " dirty weather about—that means a night at the wheel for you, Godric, old lad ! "

Godric did not mind. He loved being a sailor: he loved the sea. He loved to stand alone with the wind and the waves, his hand upon the helm : to feel the life of the ship and all on board her resting on his skill and courage, and to know that they would not fail.

For sixteen years he was a sailor. From port to port he travelled—to Scotland—Flanders—Scandinavia—and with him went his pedlar's pack. Soon he was able to buy a half-share in one merchant ship and a quarter-share in another.

" Seems our Godric is doing well," said his father.

" You wait," his mother answered, " he will do better yet."

Now, among the many places that Godric visited was the Island of Lindisfarne off the coast of Northumberland. There he saw the monastery founded by St. Aidan, talked with the monks, and saw how they lived, so differently from himself! He did not guess it at the time, but that visit was to alter his whole life, for it was there that he first heard the story of St. Cuthbert. From that moment, St. Cuthbert became his hero.

From Lindisfarne Godric went to Farne Island, where St. Cuthbert lived as a hermit, you know, and where he died. He wandered all over it—watching the waves, hearing the wild birds' cries, and thinking, thinking of St. Cuthbert.

"Selling things, sailing the seas, making money," said he to himself, "it's all *right*, but I want something else. Something different: something more—more *satisfying*." He stopped, and gazed slowly around him. Some of St. Cuthbert's birds went wheeling over his head. And suddenly—he *knew*. "I want to be like St. Cuthbert!" he cried aloud.

"Hee! Hee!" screamed the birds, scornfully. "*You'll* never be like St. Cuthbert!" But they were wrong.

Godric left Farne and Lindisfarne, but he did not go back to the sea. That part of his life was finished. A seed had been planted in his mind with the story of St. Cuthbert, and something new was to come of it, but what, he did not quite know.

In the meantime, he went on a pilgrimage to Jerusalem.

The Seed Begins to Sprout

WELL, you know how it is with seeds.   You plant them—
and nothing happens.   At least, that is what it seems like.
But something will happen presently.   You just have to
wait.

So with Godric.   He did not do anything new and
exciting at once.   He seemed just the same as before, but
his thoughts were different, and if you think differently,
sooner or later you are bound to act differently.   However,
no one noticed anything strange at first.   Except, perhaps,
his mother.

When he returned from Jerusalem, Godric took a job
as steward to a rich landowner in Norfolk.   He had not
been there long before he discovered that something was
wrong.   Some of his Master's retainers were no better
than plain thieves.

What they used to do was this.   They would pretend
to go hunting, but instead of chasing the wild deer, they
would simply steal the sheep and cattle from some peasant
or small farmer, kill them, skin them on the spot, and then
carry them home and have them served up for dinner as
venison—declaring that this was the deer they had taken
in the chase that morning.

Godric was very worried about it.   At first he only
suspected what was happening, but as soon as he was sure
he tackled the men.

It was just as they were rising from dinner one day. There had been something called venison at that dinner, but Godric had not eaten any.

"Just a moment, young sirs," said he, "I'd like a word with you."

"Well, what is it?" asked one of the young men, named Robert. "Be quick: we are in a hurry."

"I'll not keep you long," replied Godric, grimly. "Where exactly did you kill that deer we ate to-day?"

The young men looked at each other awkwardly. Two of them began, speaking at once:

"By the mill-stream——"

"In the great wood——"

then stopped, and glared at each other.

"Indeed?" said Godric. "Good hunting, that is—to kill one deer in two different places. Are you sure it *was* a deer?"

"I don't know what you are talking about," answered Robert, uneasily, edging towards the door.

But Godric stood stolidly in his way.

"Young gentlemen," said he firmly, "maybe I'm not so high born as some, nor so well learned as some, but I know the difference between venison and—beef! Now, do you swear to me never again to touch other folk's cattle or——"

"We shall do nothing of the kind," answered Robert, haughtily. "What we do is not your business, anyhow."

Godric shook his head.

"I am steward here," said he. "'Tis my place to see that all's right and honest in this house, and see to it I will, understand that! If any more of that same 'venison' comes to this table, I go to the Master."

"You can go to whom you will!" answered Robert, and swaggered out with his companions.

Godric sat down slowly, his face very grave. "I don't want to play tell-tale," he muttered, "but this is stealing, and from poor folk too, that have trouble enough to get a living, anyhow." He sighed, heavily: then slipped to his knees—" St. Cuthbert, could you tell me, please, what I should do ? "

In spite of Godric's warning, the strange venison continued to appear at the table.   At last he saw that there was no help for it—he must go to his Master.

The Master was lying back in his great chair before a blazing fire, looking very comfortable.

" Oh ! it's you, Steward," he said lazily, when Godric presented himself before him. " Well, what is it ? "

" Why, to tell you the truth, Master," began Godric heavily, " it's the venison."

" *Venison !* " exclaimed his Master, " what do you come to me for about venison ?   For whom do you take me—the cook ? "

" This is no matter for cooks, Sir," replied Godric. " A matter for the Master of the house, this is."

The Master began to look a little uneasy.

" Well ! well ! " he said, testily. " What is it then ? Out with it."

Then Godric told him the whole story.

"Nonsense," snapped the Master, when the tale was ended. " Don't believe a word of it.   Do you think I shouldn't have noticed the difference in the taste of the meat ? "

" I should have thought so, Sir, certainly," replied Godric, looking at him rather hard.

" Well, there you are then," said the Master. " If I am satisfied, what have you to worry about ?   If it comes to that," he added sharply, " you must have eaten plenty of the stuff yourself."

" So I did, Sir," admitted Godric.   " Shame and sorrow to me, so I did !   For I was not sure, and the truth is I did not want to think it was so.   But now that I am sure I eat no more of it."

" Very well, don't then ! " snapped the other.   " You can live on thistles for all I care ! "

But still Godric was not satisfied.

" Sir, won't you speak to these young men ? " he insisted.   " I've spoken in vain, but if you——"

"Oh ! be quiet, fellow ! " roared the Master. "What's the use of looking for trouble ? What comes to my table as venison *is* venison as far as I am concerned."

"In that case, Sir," said Godric gravely, "I must ask you to find another steward, for I cannot serve any longer in this house."

"Nonsense," growled the Master. "Eat what's given you, and ask no questions. Now, for goodness sake go away—you're spoiling my afternoon nap ! "

However, Godric meant what he said, and he stuck to it. He left that house. And since he knew that wrong had been done and that none of the others would make amends, he came to the conclusion that he himself must do so. He decided, therefore, to go on another pilgrimage. But where ? Godric turned the matter over in his mind— then a bright idea struck him. "Of course ! " he cried, "the very thing ! I will make pilgrimage to the Hermitage of St. Giles."

St. Giles is the patron saint of the wild deer.

So off went Godric once again, across to France, then down the River Rhone to the Hermitage of St. Giles. From there he went on to Rome, and at last came home again to his parents in England.

But not for long. The fact is, he was getting very restless. He decided to go to Rome once more.

"In that case," announced his mother, when she heard the news, "I am coming too."

"You, Mother ! " exclaimed Godric, astounded.

"The woman," remarked her husband, "is certainly mad."

"Mad I may be, or mad I may not be," answered his wife determinedly, "but I go with our Godric to Rome, and you may as well make up your mind to it."

"But why, woman ? " implored her bewildered husband.

"Why not ? " she demanded. "Other women have been on pilgrimage ! Well I know that I'm but a poor, ignorant woman, but Our Lord did not despise such——"

" Now, now," put in her husband, soothingly, " naught was said about despising. But why walk all the way to Rome when you've a comfortable home here ? "

" Because," said Godric's mother, and her eyes, that were like her son's, flashed like lightning, " because there be longings and dreamings that cannot be satisfied in a comfortable home : and because I would spend a little time with my only son before I die : and because," she added grimly, " I wish to do so ! "

Her husband sighed heavily. " Aye, woman," said he, " the last reason is enough."

But Godric said gently :

" I understand, Mother. Come with me, and welcome."

His mother put on her cloak, fastening it with great firmness, and took a bundle from the press. " I've had this ready a long time," she explained, " against the time Godric went on pilgrimage again." She kissed her husband. " There's clean linen in the press," she said, " and I've asked neighbour Beth to look to your meals. Come ! never look so forlorn ! Go I will, but I'll come back in good time."

And go she did, walking barefoot most of the way.

Now, as Godric and his mother left London they were met by another pilgrim—a lady, strangely beautiful, who asked if she might go with them.

" Come with us and welcome, my lass," said Godric's mother heartily. " It's ill travelling alone."

So the three went on together, and all the way the strange lady waited on Godric and his mother with wonderful kindness. Not till they reached Southwark on the way home did she leave them.

" If you ask me," remarked Godric's mother, as they walked on alone, " that was a saint—or even an angel."

Their pilgrimage over, Godric took his mother home again.

" Aye, but I'm glad to be back ! " she sighed, when she stood in her own kitchen. " Well, have you grown used to doing without me, husband ? "

Her husband grunted. " The clean linen," said he, " is all used up, and that Beth knows no more of cooking than a magpie ! "

Then his face broke into a broad grin of contentment.

The Full-Grown Plant

A S for Godric, he could not settle at home. He must go—where, he could not tell. He must do —what, he did not know. Only he knew that the rest of his life must be for God alone, as Saint Cuthbert's had been.

When next we hear of him he is at Penrith, wandering in and about the churches, listening to the services, trying to learn the psalms and collects by heart, and always seeking, seeking some way to be like Saint Cuthbert.

One evening, he was standing outside a church, listening to the monks inside singing a psalm, and trying to learn the words by heart, when a man coming out of the church glanced at him, hesitated, looked again, then stopped, and said :

" I seem to know your face. Aren't you called Godric —and live at Walpole, in the Fens ? "

" That's right," admitted Godric. " Why, I know you, too ! "

He had recognised the stranger as a kinsman of his father's.

They stayed talking a while. Then the stranger said :

" But what are you doing here ? "

" Well," replied Godric, " I'm—I'm learning the psalms just now," and he explained about his ambition to give up his life to God's service.

" That is a good wish," said the stranger. " I hope it

J

will come true." Then he took from his pocket a little book. It was a psalter. "Perhaps you'd like this?" said he. "It will help with the psalms. Good-bye."

Long after his kinsman had gone, Godric stood turning the book in his hands. Already it was his dearest possession.

And now at last he decided exactly what to do. Saint Cuthbert had been a hermit—he would be a hermit, too! He began at once to wander about the countryside, looking for a good place in which to start.

He was still undecided when he met a real hermit. An old man named Aelric.

"Why not begin by coming to live with me, my son?" the old man suggested, when he heard Godric's plans. "A young, strong man like you would be a great help to me. In return I will teach you all I can. It is not an easy way of life that you have chosen."

Godric agreed, and for two years he lived with the old hermit. Then Aelric died, and Godric, feeling a little unsettled again, set off on another pilgrimage.

This time he went to Jerusalem. It was his last journey abroad, and one that he never forgot, for on his way he had a vision of Saint Cuthbert. It seemed to him that his hero actually stood before him, and promised him faithfully that he should have a hermitage in England.

Feeling very pleased, Godric came back to England. It would be all right: Saint Cuthbert had promised! He went first to Durham and, just until he could find a place in which to start being a hermit properly, he took a job as bellringer at St. Giles Church. Also, he began going to school. There was one at another church in Durham —St. Mary's—and there he went to learn his letters. It was rather late in the day, perhaps, but Godric was too intent on learning to care about that. There he would sit among all the little children, learning the hymns and prayers with them.

After a time he thought he had found a place that would do for his hermitage, so he said good-bye to his friends and set off alone for the spot he had chosen. He built a little hut and lived there for a while. Then he found an even better place, so he moved, and in this second place he stayed until he died.

The spot he chose was in a hunting park on the banks of the River Wear, not far from Durham. The park belonged to Bishop Flambard, who gave him permission to settle there. The Prior of Durham undertook to look after him, and Godric promised to obey him just as if he had been one of the monks in the Priory.

At last that seed had become a full-grown plant! Godric was a hermit, like Saint Cuthbert.

He made himself a little cell to live in, and built a tiny church, which he called Saint John the Baptist's. Then he cultivated a little patch of ground, so that he could live upon the crops grown there. Apart from this, his time was all spent in praying to God, thinking of Him and worshipping Him. Except for a priest, who was sent by the Prior of Durham on Sundays and Festivals to hold a service in his little church, Godric saw scarcely anyone. If strangers did come that way, he used to hide in the bushes until they were gone.

However, there were certain people who insisted upon coming to see him. In fact, they came right into his cell without being invited! These were the Snake People. The spot where Godric had chosen to live was noted for snakes. Most people nowadays hate and fear snakes, and it was the same in Godric's time, but he rather liked them, and when they came crawling into his cell he would take them up in his hands and stroke them, admiring the beautiful patterns on their skins. The snakes seemed to like him, too, for whole swarms would come and lie by his fire. They never bit him, and two big ones used actually to curl themselves round his legs!

At last, however, there were so many that poor Godric had hardly room to sit, or kneel, or stand, or eat his dinner, and he felt he simply could not put up with it any longer. So one morning he said to them :

" My friends, I am sorry to have to say it, but you really must go. This is becoming quite too much of a good thing. If you go on like this, one of these days I shall tread upon one of you—hard. And then we shall all be sorry."

Thereupon, he unwound the two big snakes from his legs, picked the rest up in armfuls, and deposited them all gently but firmly outside.

" Now run along," said he, " and don't let us have any argument—please."

The snakes made no resistance, but obediently crawled away into the bushes and never returned again.

By this time Godric was becoming quite famous, and though he liked best to be alone, he did have visitors sometimes. Monks and priors and people like that, some of them famous themselves, would come to talk with him about all kinds of interesting and important matters, but he never told any of them who he was or where he came from.

Now, the people living in that neighbourhood were very proud of having a hermit, and they used to bring him presents. Unfortunately, these presents caused Godric quite a lot of trouble. He never kept them himself, but gave them to the poor, because he did not want to have money, or good things to eat, for fear they might take his mind off God. However, tales went round of the rich gifts received by the hermit in the park, and so thieves came to try to steal them. When they found nothing, they would often set upon Godric and beat him, thinking he had tricked them. They simply did not believe that he had given all those fine things away.

Once, he only just escaped being killed by such people. It was a party of soldiers. The Scots had invaded England and been driven back beyond the border, but some of them straggled behind the main army, and it was two or three of these who happened to find themselves near the great park in which Godric lived. Said one of them :

" I say, mates, here's a bit of luck. There's a hermit living round about here who gets all sorts of things given him. Let's see if he's got anything worth taking."

" What, him ? " sneered one of his comrades. " He won't have anything but a few mouldy old relics."

" Don't you believe it," the first answered. " I tell you, the folk round here bring him some marvellous things. I know. I used to live in these parts."

So the soldiers decided to rob Godric. They burst in upon him at dusk, as he sat reading his psalter.

" Now then, old Bag o' Bones," cried the ringleader, roughly, " out with it—everything you've got ! "

Godric rose, placed a marker in his book, closed it, and laid it quietly aside.

" I really am not worth robbing," he said, " but I don't suppose you will believe it."

They did not, but began to ransack the place, finding, of course, very little for their pains.

" I was afraid you would be disappointed," said Godric, watching them.

Then they turned upon him. Furious at finding nothing, they beat him, then twisted a stick in his hair, while the ringleader, drawing his sword, prepared to cut off his head.

" We'll teach you to cheat honest soldiers ! " he roared. " Stand ready, mates, in case he tries to make a dash for it."

But Godric made no attempt to escape. He just bent his head to receive the blow.

But it never came. Godric, kneeling there, neither angry nor afraid, but just waiting, made the soldier feel like a doll with the sawdust running out of it. If he had tried to run, or to fight, he would certainly have been killed, but he did just—nothing, and the soldier found he could not do anything either.

That is what often happens when someone really acts up to " Love your enemies." But you have to be terribly brave to do it.

The soldier flung down his sword. "Oh! come on, mates," he cried. "Not worth killing, he isn't."

So off they all went. But they took everything with them that they could carry, and the rest they destroyed before they left.

For sixty years Godric lived in his little hermitage at Finchale. His life was poor, lonely and very hard, and he loved it.

Eight years before he died he grew so ill that he could not leave his bed. Then the Prior of Durham chose two monks to look after him. One was named Reginald, and as he tended the old man he used to ask him about his past life, for like everyone else, he was dreadfully curious to know who this famous hermit really was. At first, Godric would say nothing, but gradually he began to confide in Reginald, and at last he told the whole story. Then Reginald wrote it all down, and made a book of it.

When Godric felt he was really going to die, he had himself carried into his little church and laid on the floor before the altar, and there, very peacefully and happily, he died. There, too, he was buried, just in front of the altar.

Now, after his death, pilgrims began to come to the hermitage. There were so many of them that there was no room for them all in the little church, and nowhere for them to eat and sleep. So a fine priory was built, with a large church and cells for monks to live in, and plenty of room for pilgrims, and it was called Finchale Priory.

It is all in ruins now : the monks are gone, and the pilgrims. But I think perhaps the snakes come sometimes. The great, great, great grandchildren of those that Godric knew. And they tell one another, as they slide in and out among the stones, how here was once a man who was a friend to the Snake People, and who, even when he turned them from his fireside, did it gently.

"You shall do him this kindness."

XI

SAINT THOMAS BECKET—
LONDON'S PRIDE

Thomas of London

THOMAS BECKET was his name, but he always called himself Thomas of London. And a true cockney he was, too, for he was born in Cheapside—well within the sound of Bow Bells !

His father, Gilbert Becket, was a Norman from Rouen, who had come to settle in London as a merchant, and was at one time Sheriff of London. His mother's name was Matilda. I expect you've heard that story of the Saracen maid who came all the way to England for love of Gilbert Becket, knowing only the words " Gilbert " and "London," but that, I'm afraid, is not true. Thomas's mother was a Norman, like her husband. But she was a good and lovely lady, and I'm sure neither Gilbert nor Thomas would have changed her for all the Saracens in the East.

London has always been an exciting and interesting place to live in, and so it was when Thomas was a boy. There were markets where you could buy silks and furs, jewels and armour, and many another fine thing. There were horse shows, and tournaments on land and water : hunting and hawking in the country round about : ice sports in winter, dancing in summer, fencing and archery, and even football ! If you wanted a different kind of amusement, there were poetry competitions between the schools, or plays about the Saints and Martyrs in the churches.   Thomas joined in everything and enjoyed it all thoroughly, but what he liked best was the hawking.

One day, when he was a lad, he was out hawking with a friend of his father, named Richer de l'Aigle, when he had a very narrow escape.

As the party rode along, they came to a swift stream spanned by a very narrow bridge.   It was really too narrow for a horse to cross safely, but Richer de l'Aigle managed to get over, and Thomas, who was game for anything, followed.   He was half-way over, when his horse stumbled. He tried to steady it, but it was too late.   Next moment horse and rider toppled into the river.

The current was terribly strong, and Thomas was at once swirled away downstream,. towards a place where stood a mill with its millrace, turning the great waterwheel. If once he reached that there would be no hope for him— he would be dashed to pieces on the wheel in no time.

Richer de l'Aigle and his attendants galloped frantically along the bank, shouting to each other to do something. But no one had a rope : there were no boats : no swimmer could fight against that rushing torrent.   Helplessly they watched Thomas being carried along like a cork on the water.

Suddenly, something astonishing happened. The wheel stopped turning !   Then, while they blinked in amazement, they saw the miller come out of his house and proceed to pull Thomas out of the water. With a shout, Richer de l'Aigle galloped to the spot. When he arrived, he found Thomas lying half drowned on the bank, with the miller bending over him. The rest of the party soon joined them, and between them all they managed to bring the boy round. It was not until they were quite sure he was all right, and they had all had time to think about what had happened, that someone exclaimed :

" But the wheel stopped !   Miller, what made you stop the wheel ?   You couldn't have *seen*——"

The miller thoughtfully scratched his head. " Seemed to me," he said slowly, " as if I had to."   He looked down at Thomas, now almost recovered. " Just as if I were told to——" he added.

There was an awed silence. Then someone whispered : " A miracle ! "

It certainly was very strange.

But Thomas did not spend all his time hawking or looking at the fine things in London town. Like other boys, he had to go to school. He went first to Merton Priory, in Surrey : then to one of the best schools in London, and afterwards to Paris.

It was while he was at Merton that Prior Robert, the head of the Priory, one day discovered Gilbert Becket kneeling before his son. The Prior did not approve of that at all.

" Come ! Come ! " he exclaimed, " This won't do. A father kneeling to his son ! It should be the other way round."

Gilbert rose from his knees, but said nothing. As for Thomas, he felt dreadfully awkward.

Afterwards, when they were alone, Gilbert said to the Prior.

" I couldn't explain just now why I was kneeling to Thomas like that, but I knew what I was doing. Some day, that boy is going to be great—not just ordinary greatness—but great in the sight of God."

He did not live to see it, for both he and his wife died while Thomas was still a young man, but the Prior, who was Thomas's friend all his life, and later his Confessor, saw Gilbert's words come true.

By the time he was twenty-two, Thomas had finished his education. He came back from Paris a tall, slim, handsome young man with dark hair and bright, piercing eyes, a very pleasant, attractive manner, and the most beautiful hands.

Now he had to make his way in the world.

His father's friend, Richer de l'Aigle, gave him a job as his Notary or Secretary for about six months : then he was clerk to the Sheriff's Court for two years or so.

But his career did not really begin until he entered the household of the Archbishop of Canterbury. The Archbishop—his name was Theobald—had known Thomas's father well, for they were both Normans—in fact they had been neighbours when they lived in Normandy—so it was not surprising that he should be willing to give the son of his old friend a chance.

Thomas was twenty-four when he went to join the household of the Archbishop, and from the first he did well. All the same, it's a wonder that he stayed, for it was there that he met one of his bitterest enemies. This was Roger de Pont l'Eveque. He was a very ambitious person and he was probably jealous because the Archbishop made rather a fuss of Thomas. Very likely he was afraid Thomas would get some high position that he himself wanted. Whatever the reason, he teased and persecuted Thomas so much that his life became a perfect misery. Twice he was driven away by this man's behaviour, but each time the Archbishop persuaded him to come back, and at last he settled down.

For twelve years Thomas was a member of the Archbishop's household, and before they were over, Roger had good reason to be jealous, for the Archbishop thought so highly of Thomas that he gave him all his most important business to attend to, and even took him to Rome with him on various important missions. After a while (having first been to Italy to do some more studying), he was ordained a deacon, and finally he became Archdeacon of Canterbury. This was the very position which his old enemy, Roger de Pont l'Eveque had held, but as he was now Archbishop of York, he had nothing to grumble about this time.

Now, in 1154, a new king came to the throne of England. This was Henry II, and Henry II needed a Chancellor.

" May I suggest Thomas Becket, Your Majesty ? " said the Archbishop of Canterbury.

" That's a splendid idea ! " exclaimed Henry.

So it was arranged. Thomas became Chancellor of England.

The Archbishop was pleased—he thought it would be good for everyone if the King had a man like Thomas at his side. The King was pleased—he had taken a great fancy to Thomas. Thomas himself was not so sure. He liked the idea in a way, but he knew some of the other great men in the country would be jealous, and that he would soon have a lot of enemies. He was right. They were, and he did.

Thomas the Great Man

HOWEVER, he found plenty of friends, too, and he made a very magnificent Chancellor.

He was always giving presents—hardly a day passed but somebody said to somebody else, " Look what the Chancellor gave me ! "   His house was open to all, and everyone who came to Court was welcome at his table.   Though he ate very plain food himself, for his guests there were gold and silver dishes full of the loveliest things to eat, with rare wines to drink with them.   And no stinting, either, but as much as they wanted for everyone.   You read about tables " groaning " with luxuries sometimes.   Thomas's table simply never stopped groaning !

As for the rest of his housekeeping—he had so many fine horses, so many knights and squires and pages, so many fine clothes for himself and his servants, that he even outshone the King himself, and when he went to France to arrange about a marriage between Henry's son and the French King's daughter, he went in such splendour that the French people could hardly believe their eyes. " If this is the Chancellor's state," they cried, " what must the King's be like ? "

But it was not the presents, or the fine things to eat, or anything of that kind that brought Thomas his friends and made the people love him. It was what an old writer calls his " courtesy of the heart." His real kindness, and helpfulness and consideration for others.

One of Thomas's best friends was the King himself. Thomas was about fifteen years older then the King, but he was not a bit old in his ways, and he and the King were great friends from the first, popping in and out of each other's house just when they felt like it, and romping about in public like a couple of schoolboys.

Once, as they were riding through the streets together, they saw a poor old man creeping along just ahead of them.

" Look at that old chap ! " exclaimed the King. " How poor he is ! And he's hardly got any clothes on. Wouldn't it be kind to give him a nice warm cloak ? "

Thomas, with a sly smile, answered :

" Your cloak, Sire, would be just the very thing."

But the King ignored that. Beckoning to the old fellow, he said : " Could you do with a cloak, my man ? "

The poor old chap only gaped at him. This was a great lord—he could see that—but he had no idea it was the King himself. As for answering his question—of course he could do with a new cloak, but then he could do with a great many things he saw no chance of getting. Too bewildered to answer, he stood silent, twisting his tattered cap in his hands.

Suddenly, Henry swung round to Thomas, crying : " You shall do him this kindness ! " and snatched at his cape.   Thomas laughingly resisted, and there was quite a little struggle between them—all in the best of tempers—until Thomas gave way and let the King take his cape from him.

"Here you are, my man!" cried Henry, flinging it to the beggar in a lordly fashion. "With best wishes from the Chancellor!"

Clutching his treasure, the old man scuttled off, praising God loudly for this unexpected piece of good fortune, while Thomas sat gazing after his cape with a rather rueful smile.

A perfectly new cape it was—scarlet and grey.

However, of course Thomas had other things to do beside giving banquets and having fun with the King.   He had a very high, important and responsible position.   King Henry was full of plans for improving the laws of England and for other reforms, and in all these, Thomas was his right hand man.

He did his share of fighting too.   Partly in Wales, and partly in France, when the King sent an army to try to win back Toulouse which was claimed by his wife, Queen Eleanor.   Seven hundred knights followed Thomas then, and he proved as good a general as he was a Chancellor.

But all this was only a beginning.   The most important part of Thomas's life was yet to come.   It began when he was made Archbishop of Canterbury.

He did not want to be Archbishop.   When someone suggested it to him, he said quickly: "I know at least three poor priests in Canterbury, any one of whom would make a better Archbishop than I."

When the King mentioned it, Thomas told him it would mean trouble between them.

"If I am Archbishop, you and I will quarrel, Your Majesty," said he, sadly.   "I know we shall."

But the King would not take any notice.   He wanted Thomas to be Archbishop.   Archbishop Theobald, now dead, had wanted it also.   As for what Thomas had said about quarrelling—the King did not think he really meant it.

But he did.   He knew quite well what would happen. He knew that the King wanted to make some new laws and alter old ones, so that the Church in England would not have so much power, and the King would have more. But Thomas thought that was wrong.   He thought the Church should not be interfered with by any king.   That might not have mattered if he had still been Chancellor, but if he were Archbishop of Canterbury, he would have to say so, and, as head of the Church in England, he would feel it his duty to fight against the changes the King wanted to make.   And then—well—then there would be trouble.

However, the King insisted, Thomas at last gave in, and in due course he was elected Archbishop of Canterbury.

Much to the surprise of many people, he at once seemed to change completely.   Instead of splendid clothes, he wore a plain black cassock with a hair shirt beneath it.   Instead of laughing and talking, he sat silent at the table, though he liked his guests to be as lively as before.   He had always lived on rather plain food, but now he ate little but bread, and water in which hay had been boiled.   He had always been good at giving presents—now he gave away twice as much as even Archbishop Theobald had ever done.

Every day he invited thirteen beggars to his cell, washed their feet, in remembrance of Our Lord, and gave them money.   He visited the sick, looked after the widows and orphans, and spent much of his time in planning what he could do for the old and infirm monks of Canterbury.

The people began to love him even better as Archbishop than they had done as Chancellor.

But the trouble which Thomas had expected was not far off.   It began when he resigned his position as Chancellor.   The King did not like that at all.

" I don't see why you can't be both," he said.

" Don't you ? " said Thomas.

" No, I don't.   That was my whole idea."

" I'm sorry about that," replied Thomas, quietly, " but you see, it just won't work."

So this time it was the King who had to give in.

Thomas would be Archbishop of Canterbury or Chancellor of England. He would not be both. Still, although the King was disappointed, they did not actually quarrel—yet.

But it was not very long before they did, for almost at once King Henry began to try to carry out his plans, which Thomas resisted. Then, after a great deal of argument, the King drew up a set of laws called The Constitutions of Clarendon, setting out what the Church could and could not do. Thomas would not agree to these at first : then he did : then he thought better of it, and refused to set his seal upon them.

Now the King became really angry. He determined to get the better of Thomas at all costs. A chance soon came. It happened that a man named John the Marshall was having a lawsuit over some property. It was first tried in the Archbishop's Court, but when things seemed to be going against him, he said it was not fair, and demanded to have the case tried again at Westminster. This was agreed to, and Thomas was called to Westminster, but he did not go, partly because he was ill. Then a Council of Bishops and Barons was called at Northampton, and Thomas was commanded to appear before it.

"Ah-ha !" said the King to himself, "*now* I've got him !"

And instead of sticking to the point about John the Marshall, he began to accuse Thomas of all sorts of things, especially of misusing money while he was Chancellor. Some people even whispered that he had called Thomas a traitor.

Well, the Council went on and on for days—but at last the old Earl of Leicester stood up to deliver judgment.

But Thomas would not hear it. "I have had no trial," said he, "I will hear no judgment," and carrying his cross, he walked out of the hall.

"Traitor !" "Perjurer !" cried his enemies, as he passed among them.

But when he reached the street, a great crowd of people knelt for his blessing.

K

Hardly had Thomas left the Council, than someone sent word secretly that some of his enemies were planning to kill him. He was no coward, but there was no point in sitting waiting to be killed. He decided to leave England.

He went from Sandwich, in Kent, to Flanders, travelling disguised as a novice. It was a very different journey from the time when he went to France in such splendour. Then, he rode with two hundred knights behind him : now he had to walk, or when the rain made the roads too bad, to ride on a hired horse with a rope bridle and a saddle made from his own clothes. Then, all the people came running out to see him : now, nobody took any notice of him at all.

Except a certain innkeeper and his wife. She noticed him first.

" We've got *company* this day, husband," she whispered, as she bustled about, serving the guests.

" Well, and don't I know it," he answered irritably. " Run off my legs I am with them ! "

" It's one special one I'm talking about," his wife answered. " Ah ! he's company, and no mistake. Look —him over there in the corner."

" What ? " snorted the innkeeper, " that novice ? "

" Novice ! " his wife was unutterably scornful. " Novice indeed ! Have a good look at him—*look at his hands*."

The innkeeper strolled over to the stranger in the corner. " Did you ever see the like ? " whispered his wife, when he rejoined her. " There's only one person with hands like those, and that's——"

" What ? " he gasped. " You don't mean——"

His wife nodded. " Yes. *The Archbishop of Canterbury*."

Just then some poor children came sneaking into the inn, in the hope of begging a few scraps of food from the tables. Most of the guests turned away, but the " novice " beckoned to them. There was something about the kind, gracious way in which he gave them the little food he had, that quite convinced the innkeeper.

"Wife," said he, "you're right. The hands *might* pass, but nobody save Thomas of London has such a way with the little ones."

When the other guests were gone, he and his wife spoke to Thomas. They were quite overwhelmed at having him at their inn, and they gave him food for his journey. Very humble food it was, just apples, cheese and peas, but Thomas was very glad of it.

So he went on, sometimes riding, sometimes walking until at last he reached the Hermitage of Saint Bertimus, and there he was joined by his friend Herbert of Bosham and some more of his clerks and servants, bringing horses, clothes and other things from Canterbury.

From there they went on to Sens, where Thomas saw the Pope and told him all his troubles, and so at last the little party of exiles came to the great Cistercian Monastery at Pontigny. There, for a while, they stayed.

All this time the King was getting more and more angry. He was also rather frightened in case Thomas should excommunicate him. So he did a dreadfully mean thing. He could not touch Thomas, but he banished all his relations. Many of them were old, simple people who knew nothing about the quarrel with the King, and some were little babies. The King banished them all, and with them some of Thomas's friends who had stood up for him.

"They are all traitors," he cried, "who have not the zeal or the courage to rid me of the trouble of this one man."

For seven years Thomas stayed on the Continent, and all this time the quarrel continued, with everyone in England, and many important people in Europe, taking sides : with King Henry getting more angry, and Thomas more determined. At last, after two or three tries, they patched up a kind of peace, and Thomas agreed to return to England. But, though he and the King were supposed to be friends, in his heart of hearts he knew that things would never be the same again.

Thomas the Martyr

O once more Thomas arrived at Sandwich—this time travelling *to* England.   He received a tremendous welcome.   Crowds came to greet him, and all the way to Canterbury the roads were lined with people who threw their clothes and even themselves before him.

At Canterbury the whole town turned out in their best clothes to welcome him.   The Cathedral was decorated and a procession met him and brought him, with hymns and solemn music, to his palace, and a state banquet was given in his honour.   But still he knew that the trouble was not over.

He was very soon proved right.   The Archbishop of York (that same Roger de Pont l'Eveque who had always been his enemy) actually told the King's son, Henry, that Thomas was plotting against him!   It was not true, of course, and Thomas rode at once to London to tell the Prince so.   But the Prince would not even see him, and sent word commanding him to go back to Canterbury and stay there.   Very much surprised and hurt (for the Prince had been brought up in his household and he had been very good to him), Thomas returned home.

But worse was soon to follow.   Three of Thomas's most bitter enemies, determined to make mischief, went to the King, who was still on the Continent, with a long story of all the awful things Thomas was doing.   They declared he was going round England at the head of a large body of armed men, and did all they could to stir up the King against him.

" Well," snapped Henry, " what do you suggest I should do about it ? "

" My Lord," said the Archbishop of York (you can guess he was one of the three), " My Lord, while Thomas lives, you will not have peace or quiet to see another good day."

It was almost like suggesting that the King should have him murdered. Henry did not go quite so far as that, but he lost his temper so badly, crying out that it was wasting food and drink to give it to people who called themselves his friends but would not avenge him on " this low clerk," that it was no wonder those who heard him thought he would be pleased if the deed were done.

You know what happened : Four knights, Reginald FitzUrse, William de Tracy, Hugh de Morville and Richard Brito, secretly set out for England. They meant to kill Thomas, and they imagined that the King would be delighted.

But when the King heard that they had gone, he guessed what they meant to do, and like a good many people who lose their tempers and say things they don't quite mean, he was frightened and wished he hadn't. He hastily sent orders that Thomas was to be arrested, and that the knights were not to do anything drastic. But the knights took no notice. Perhaps the command never reached them.

Instead, they collected some followers and rode on to Canterbury. It was just after dinner when they arrived. Thomas was busy in an inner room, but his attendants received the knights in quite a friendly way.

" Will you have some dinner ? " they asked. " We've only just finished."

The knights scornfully refused. They insisted on seeing the Archbishop.

" Very well," said Thomas quietly, when he was told. " I will go out to them." He dismissed his monks and went to see the waiting knights alone. But as the monks filed out of the room, the doorkeeper whispered : " Stand by a minute. This looks like trouble."

Meanwhile, Thomas had joined the knights in the other

room. At first they would not speak, but stood and looked at him grimly.

"What can I do for you, gentlemen?" asked Thomas.

"We must speak to you privately," they answered roughly.

"Oh! no," Thomas answered quietly. "What you have to say must be said in public."

That made them angry, and it was a good thing that the monks were near, for they rushed in only just in time to stop one of the knights trying to strike Thomas with his own cross.

Then they began to accuse him of every kind of wickedness. Thomas denied everything. At last, when they saw that he was not to be frightened they began to be a little nervous themselves. So one of them said:

"Well, we come from the King, and his command is that you leave the country at once with all your followers."

This was not true. He had made it up, thinking perhaps that it would do if, instead of actually killing him, they just drove him from the country.

But Thomas refused to go. "I shall stay in England even if it costs me my life," he assured them.

"Very well," said the knights. "You stay here at the risk of your life then."

"Why? Do you come to kill me?" asked Thomas. "I'm not afraid of your threats. I'm as willing to die as you are to kill me."

The knights did not answer. After a moment they turned and strode out of the room. Thomas followed them to the door. "Here—here you shall find me," he said, and touched his neck as much as to say "that's the place to strike at."

The moment the knights had gone, Thomas's monks clustered round him, begging and imploring him to seek safety in the Cathedral. He refused, and tried to comfort them, but they were past taking comfort, even from him, and in spite of his protests they began frantically to drag and hustle him towards the Cathedral.

Meanwhile, the four knights had collected some more followers to back them up, and armed with various weapons with which to force their way in, they came back to the Archbishop's palace. They found the doors barred, but discovered a wooden partition which they managed to break down. This led them to the cloisters and so to the doors of the Cathedral itself.

But these doors also were barred. They listened: inside, they could hear the priests singing vespers.

"He's here. I'll swear he's here," muttered one of the knights.

"Bang on the door," said another.

They began to beat furiously upon the doors.

Inside, stood Thomas, surrounded by a crowd of terrified monks, and the priests who had been singing vespers.

Crash! Crash! sounded upon the great doors. The monks had been in such a hurry to fasten them that they had left some of their own people outside.

"Open the doors," commanded Thomas. "It is not fitting to make a fortress of the house of prayer. We did not come to resist, but to suffer." And he himself went to the door and opened it. "Come in," he called to the monks who had been left outside. "Quicker! quicker!"

They scuttled in like a lot of frightened fowls, and after them surged the four knights and their followers.

"Where is Thomas Becket, traitor to the King and realm?" they cried. There was no answer. (Thomas was not going to answer to the name of traitor.)

The knights peered about the Cathedral. I'm sorry to say that all except three of Thomas's people had run away, or hidden. Those three, his Confessor, his Secretary, and a monk named Thomas Grimm had persuaded Thomas to go up some steps leading to the choir, where they thought his enemies might not see him, for it was already getting dark. But Thomas had no intention of hiding.

"Where is the Archbishop?" cried the knights, and this time Thomas answered them.

" I am no traitor," he said.   " Why do you seek me ? "

He came down the stairs, and stood between two altars. The knights followed, shouting and threatening, their voices echoing through the vast Cathedral.

Again Thomas defied them.

" Then you shall die," cried the knights, " and get what you deserve."

Thomas answered :

" I am ready to die for my Lord that in my blood the Church may obtain liberty and peace.   But do not dare to harm any of my people," he added, sternly.

And still the knights hesitated.   Even they did not quite fancy killing Thomas there in the Cathedral.   Instead, they tried to carry him off as their prisoner, but Thomas would not come, and when Reginald FitzUrse got too near, he pushed him away·quite roughly.

Then that knight rushed upon him, waving his sword above his head.

" *It's come*," thought Thomas, and, bending his head, began to pray.

Again Reginald FitzUrse sprang upon him, and this time he struck him a terrible blow on the crown of his head.   Edward Grimm tried to stop it, and nearly got his arm cut off.

But Thomas was not an easy person to kill.   Three times they struck him before he fell.   Then, as he lay there, one of them struck him again, so hard that the sword was broken, and that was the end.   Thomas Becket was dead.

One of those who had come with the knights put his foot on Thomas's neck.   " Let us away, knights," he cried. " He will rise no more."

Shouting : " The King's men !   The King's men ! " the knights rushed out of the church and galloped away, and as they rode through Canterbury a thunderstorm broke over the city.

People crowded into the Cathedral, for rumours of the fight had begun to spread.   They found Thomas's body lying where his enemies had left it, and for a long while no one dared to touch it.

The people of England had always loved Thomas. Now they hailed him at once as a Saint. Tales were told of his miracles: first at Canterbury: then all over England: then on the Continent. Soon, the first of the Canterbury Pilgrims set out to visit his shrine.

Meanwhile, King Henry, full of grief and repentance (now that it was too late), was dressing himself in sackcloth and pouring ashes on his head. For three days he remained alone, refusing to eat or be comforted. The Pope, having excommunicated the murderers of Thomas and all who had helped them, punished the King, too, with many penances, and when he came to England he did penance again at Thomas's shrine.

Thomas was buried in the Cathedral crypt at first. There he lay until 1220 when his body was solemnly moved to a splendid new shrine in the Cathedral itself, a shrine which the people of England insisted should be made of nothing less than gold.

Perhaps it was a pity that they insisted on gold, for of course, when Henry VIII came along he soon laid hands on it. The golden shrine was destroyed, and Thomas's relics were burnt and the ashes scattered to the wind.

But I think you can still find Saint Thomas in Canterbury Cathedral.

"Drop them in there," said Hugh.

XII

SAINT HUGH OF LINCOLN

Motherless

"AND what's going to happen about me, Father ? " enquired Hugh. " I can't stay here all alone "—he gulped back a sob —" without mother *or* you ! "

Count William of Avalon smiled down at his youngest son. " William and Peter will be here," he reminded him.

Hugh—he was barely ten years old—cast a look of lofty scorn at his two big brothers. " William and Peter are no use," he said.

It was a sad little party that was gathered that day in the great hall of the Castle of Avalon, in Savoy, for the Count's wife, the Countess Anna, was dead. How he and his three sons were to get on at Avalon without her none of them could imagine, in fact the Count had decided that he just could not do it. He had been telling them his plans, as they sat round the fire together. William and Peter, who were already grown up, were to have the castle and estates between them. He himself would spend the rest of his life quietly in a monastery. It was then that Hugh had looked up and demanded :

" What's going to happen about me ? "

His father drew the boy close against him. " It's all right, Hugh," said he. " You are coming to the monastery, too."

Hugh considered this idea gravely. " Yes," he said at

163

last, " I should like that."   He wriggled from his father's arms.   " I had better be getting ready," he said importantly. " Am I to ride my pony ? "

The Lord of Avalon shook his head.   " We are going to walk, Hugh.   We are not to be great folk any more, you and I, but poor and humble—like the good monks."

Hugh paused on his way to the door.

" I wish to be a monk myself," he announced firmly.

So if you had been living about the year 1150 and had happened to be travelling near Grenoble, you might have met them, a sad-looking elderly gentleman, striding along hand in hand with a sturdy little boy.

The monastery they went to was called Villarbenoit. The monks there welcomed them warmly and they soon felt quite at home.

You might think a monastery would be rather a serious place for a little boy of ten, but no, Hugh had a fine time. There were a lot of other boys there—some who were to be monks, and others, the sons of noblemen, who had been sent there to be educated.   Hugh soon made friends, and joined in everything with the greatest eagerness. Between their lessons the boys played plenty of noisy, jolly games, and Hugh would run and jump and wrestle with the best, until the old priest who was the schoolmaster, and who knew that both Hugh and his father wanted the boy to be a monk, would get rather worried.

" Hughie, Hughie," he would say, " I'm bringing you up for Christ—those things are not for you."

But he need not have worried—Hugh was a fine little fellow.   The rough play toughened his body : it could not spoil his character.

Hugh did so well at Villarbenoit that when he was only fifteen he was allowed to take his vows and become a real monk.   Now he, like all the others, would have some special work to do, but first he had to go and ask the Prior what it was to be.

" Of course," he thought to himself, as he made his way to the Prior's cell that first morning, " I'll do anything *gladly*.   Only I do hope it will be something that will leave me time to keep Father company sometimes."

The Prior greeted him very kindly.   Like everyone else at Villarbenoit, he had a soft spot for Hugh.

" Well now," said he, " about your work, my son." He paused, looking at Hugh very gravely, till Hugh began to wonder whatever was coming.   Then, suddenly, he smiled.   " Your work," said he, " will be to care for your father for the rest of his life."

Hugh's heart gave a great leap of joy.

" But that's not *work !* " he burst out.

So for the next few years Hugh was his father's servant, nurse and companion.   He did everything for him, and did it so well that by the time the Count died he was as good as a trained nurse.   From then on, anyone who had Hugh to look after them might consider themselves very lucky.

But Hugh's next work was something very different. He was about nineteen, and had not long been made a deacon, when the Prior sent for him and said :

" My son, I want you to preach a course of sermons in the Priory Church."

" I, Father ! " exclaimed Hugh, " but—but I don't think I could.   I—I'm not very old—and I haven't been a deacon very long——"

" All the same," interrupted the Prior, " I want you to try."

" Very well, Father," answered Hugh, obediently.   But secretly he felt quite scared.

He went on feeling frightened right up to the day when he was to preach his first sermon.   It was not as if he had just to preach to the other monks.   There would be strangers there, people living round about who liked to come to the monastery church.   Supposing he forgot what he was going to say ?   Supposing his voice just wouldn't come ?   Supposing—" Oh ! *dear*," sighed Hugh.

At last the time came.   Feeling more frightened than ever, Hugh stood up to begin his sermon.   And suddenly

—it was quite all right !   He forgot everything except the things he wanted to say and the people to whom he was speaking.   Everyone said it was the best sermon they had ever heard, and from that time, whenever Hugh preached the church was packed.   By the time he had finished the course he was quite famous.

It was not long before the Prior had some more special work for him.   Not far away there was a little Priory called St. Maximin, which was attached to Villarbenoit. Whoever looked after it had to act as parish priest for the district.   One day the Prior told Hugh that he was to go and take charge of St. Maximin's.

Hugh was even more alarmed than he had been about the sermons.

" But, Father," he protested, " I'm not even a priest. How can I possibly do this work ? "

" With God's help, my son," answered the Prior.   " As all good work is done."

" But won't He think I'm taking rather too much upon myself ? " ventured Hugh.   " Really, I don't feel I dare——"

But the Prior was firm.   " Nonsense," said he. " You'll manage splendidly."

" Well then," said Hugh, seeing there was no help for it, " couldn't I have someone older—a priest perhaps—to administer the Sacraments and advise me about things ?"

To this the Prior agreed.   An old priest was chosen to go with him, and with his help and advice Hugh made a great success of his new work.   It was in a very poor place, and what with preaching and visiting the many poor folk round about, he had plenty to do.

Yet, after a time he began to be dissatisfied.   You'll never guess the reason.   He thought his life was too easy !

Have you ever trained for something special ?   Perhaps for the school sports, or to pass an examination ?   If so, you will know that to succeed you have to give up a lot of easy and comfortable things which don't go with winning races and passing examinations.   Well, Hugh was training to be the best possible kind of Christian, and easy and comfortable things don't go with that, either.   So he looked about for somewhere where he could live a hard, plain, simple life, without any of those things in it which might make him give up bothering to be good and just be comfortable.

He found what he wanted at the Monastery of Grande Chartreuse.   The monks there were called Carthusians.   A monk's life is not an easy one at any time, but to be a Carthusian monk you need to be as tough as a Commando. The Monastery stood high up in the Alps.   The scenery was grand, but goodness, how bleak and wild it was, and how cold in the winter ! In spite of that, the monks wore just a hair shirt with a rough habit over it, while for bedclothes they had only a horse cloth and a sheep skin.

Then there was the loneliness.   Each monk lived in a separate little house of his own, with a small garden, and only met the others in church at the services, or on Sundays and Holy Days when they had meals together.   They were only allowed to talk to each other once a week.

Most of their time was spent in copying books, or in carpentry, gardening or something of that kind.   Once a week they had to take a walk in the mountains for the sake of exercise, and to refresh their minds, and if you've ever seen the Alps you'll agree that there could not be a better place for both.

It was this hard and lonely life that Hugh set his heart upon.   At Villarbenoit they did not at all want him to go, but at last he managed it.   One day, he set out alone, and came to Grande Chartreuse.

He had to begin right from the beginning, and at first it was very hard, especially the loneliness, for he was a friendly person, but gradually he grew to like it.   Though he had no human beings for company, the birds and squirrels used to pop in and out of his house just like neighbours, and in the end he was as happy as he had dreamed of being.

After a while he was made a priest.   About this time he was given the care of a very old monk, and he looked after him just as he had looked after his own father, until the old man died.

His next work was very different. He was made Procurator or Bursar of the Monastery. This meant that he had to look after the lay brothers, and also any guests who came to the Monastery. The lay brothers lived in the Monastery precincts but were not monks. They worked as farmers, shepherds, or at some trade, for at Grande Chartreuse they made everything they needed for themselves. As for the guests, there were always travellers coming and going, or monks visiting from other monasteries, or folk who wanted to spend a little time away from all the hurry and bustle of the world, thinking and praying.

Hugh was just the person for this kind of work, because he liked *people*. He was never too high and mighty for the humble ones, yet he was clever enough to talk with the clever ones. He was sorry for the bad ones, patient with the rough ones, and gentleness itself with the sick and sorry ones. He was as pleased, when anyone told him of a piece of good fortune, as if it had been his own, but if anyone was in trouble there was no one like him for sympathy. He could crack a joke, bind up a wound, or get a baby to sleep, and all without ever losing his temper or seeming in a hurry. So people began to talk about him, when they talked of their travels. " Ever been to Grande Chartreuse ? " someone would ask. " There's a monk there— Brother Hugh of Avalon—marvellous chap—" and another would break in—" I know ! I was there in the spring with my sons. A rough journey it was, and one of them was a bit done up, but Brother Hugh soon put him to rights ! Splendid, he was. Nothing too much trouble. And so *jolly*. Yes, he's a great fellow—Hugh of Avalon."

So Hugh's fame spread far and wide, for his guests came from all parts of the continent. It spread even as far as England, and that was the beginning of a most unexpected change in his life.

Henry II was ruling England then. Thomas Becket had been murdered (all through Henry losing his temper)

and the King, who was terribly sorry, and still more
terribly frightened, had vowed to build three monasteries
to make up for it.   But when he had got over his fright a
little he began to wish he hadn't because first he didn't
want to give up any land to build them on, and second,
where was the money coming from ?   He managed two,
but still another was wanted.

"Bother," said the King.   "Well, they must just have
Witham and do the best they can."

So he made a grant of land at Witham in Somerset to
a small group of Carthusian monks—and left it at that.

The monks moved in, but as the King had given them
no money at all they could not build themselves a monastery, and were obliged to live in little huts made of twigs.
But this was not the worst.   There were people already
living on that land—serfs and small farmers whose fathers
and grandfathers had lived in the same little wooden huts,
tilling the same ground or driving their cattle to feed on
the very same pastures for hundreds of years.   To them,
the monks seemed like robbers come to take the little that
they had, and they would neither sell them food nor help
them in any way.   In fact, they treated them so badly that
the first Prior of that little community ran away, and the
second fell ill and died.

Now, King Henry hadn't much wanted to start a
monastery at Witham, but when he found that the people
were trying to prevent him, he made up his mind that he
just would.

"Only, how am I going to manage ?" he asked, " if
these Priors all give up so easily ? "   He was visiting his
estates in France at the time and had been telling some of
the gentlemen there about his troubles.

It was the Count of Maurienne who answered.

"Why not ask Brother Hugh of Avalon to be Prior of
Witham, Your Majesty ? " he suggested.

The King looked doubtful.

"A foreigner ? " said he.   "That's not likely to
improve matters."

L

"It wouldn't make any difference with Hugh of Avalon," replied the Count. "He never seems like a foreigner to anyone, whatever nationality they are. You see, he never bothers about it himself. To him, people are—well—just *people*. And he seems to love people— good, bad and indifferent. Believe me, Your Majesty, if anyone can make your new monastery a success it will be Hugh of Avalon."

"Then get him—get him—get him!" commanded the King.

So from England a deputation set out, led by Reginald, Bishop of Bath, to the Grande Chartreuse, to ask Hugh to be Prior of Witham. They knew it was going to be difficult to persuade the Prior of Grande Chartreuse to spare him, so to be on the safe side they asked the Archbishop of Grenoble to go with them and help.

When the message was delivered to Hugh he could hardly believe his ears. He was forty years old and had quite expected to spend the rest of his life at Grande Chartreuse.

"But I can't even govern my own soul for a single day!" he exclaimed. "How can I possibly go to a strange land to govern the souls of others? Let someone else go and the King will get a better bargain than he expects."

But the deputation would not be put off. "No," they said. "It must be Hugh—and Hugh alone."

Nobody at Grande Chartreuse liked the idea at all. The Prior did not want it, the monks did not want it, and Hugh did not want it himself. They called a meeting to discuss the matter, and they would very likely have refused King Henry's request, but for the Archbishop of Grenoble, who pointed out that here was a work of great importance which Hugh would certainly do well. He ought, said the Archbishop, to undertake it.

Hugh could do nothing but obey. Very reluctantly, he rolled up his few belongings in his old horsecloth, and set off for England.

The New Prior

Down at Witham, in Somerset, the people were full of the
latest gossip.

" They do say," announced the Oldest Inhabitant,
" that there be another of they Priors coming."

" Let 'un come ! " cried his grandson—a sturdy young
fellow. " We'll make short work of he ! Robbers and
knaves they be—they monks—all of 'em ! "

A woman spoke up, enjoying the thought of the
excitement she was going to cause.

" Prior be here already," she said. " I've seen 'un."

" Eh ? " they crowded round her. " What's he like ? "
they demanded.

The woman considered.

" Seems he do look a kindly soul," she said slowly.

Her words were greeted with scorn and anger.

" Robbers   and   knaves ! "   shouted   the   peasants.
" Robbers and knaves, all of 'em ! "

Meanwhile, the monks were showing Hugh round his
new home, and the more he saw of it the less he liked it.

" But we cannot live long in these little huts ! " he
exclaimed.

" Oh ! they are only temporary," the monks assured
him hastily.

" They look *extremely* temporary," replied Hugh. " We

must see about building ourselves a better home as soon as possible.   What about money ? ”

The monks shook their heads.   His Majesty had made no arrangement about that.

“ I see.   And what about the peasants ? ” continued Hugh.   “ If we build here they will have to move.   Has other land been given them ? ”

The monks shook their heads.   His Majesty had made no arrangement about *that*.

“ It seems to me,” said Hugh, a trifle grimly, “ that I had better go and have a word with His Majesty.”

So to the Court came Hugh and stood before the King. He did not beat about the bush, but told His Majesty straight out that the peasants now living on the land on which the new monastery was to be built must have other land in its place.   Henry, rather grudgingly, agreed.   Very well—they should have land elsewhere. It should be arranged at once.

But if he thought that settled everything, he was mistaken.

“ Now, about the peasants’ houses, Your Majesty,” Hugh went on briskly. “ I thought perhaps you would like to buy them.”

“ Me—buy them ? ” exclaimed the King.   “ Whatever for ? ”

“ Well,” said Hugh, “ the people will have to have houses where they are going, and they certainly won’t be able to afford to build them unless they are paid for those they leave behind.”

The King waved his hand as though he were wafting the problem clean out of the window.

“ That’ll be all right,” said he, airily.   “ They’ll manage.”

“ I am sorry, Sire,” said Hugh, firmly, “ but I cannot possibly take possession of this land if the people are to suffer.”   He looked the King squarely in the eyes. “ That,” said he, “ is quite certain.”

The King could hardly believe his ears.   This was

something quite different from what he had been used to. His idea was that he should be the one to say : " I cannot possibly," while everyone else answered meekly : " Yes, Your Majesty " or " No, Your Majesty."   And now, here was this person, who was only a monk—and a foreigner at that—telling him that *he* " could not possibly ! " " I— I've a great mind to—to——" thought the King.   Then he looked again at Hugh, and somehow he thought better of it.

" Oh ! all right then," he said, rather sulkily.   " I'll buy them."

" Thank you, Sire," said Hugh, smiling.   " Now," he added, " see what a rich man I've made you—all those houses of your very own ! "

" Huh ! " grunted the King.   " You'll ruin me, that's what you'll do if you go on like this.   What on earth is the use of all those peasants' huts to me ? "

At that, Hugh had a bright idea.   Quick as a flash he answered :

" Well, Sire, if you don't want them, won't you give them to me ?   I haven't a house at all, you know."

" No house ? " cried the King.   " Why, I'm giving you a splendid great monastery !   What do you want with these miserable little shacks as well ? "

But Hugh was too clever to tell the King just what he did want with them.   He simply answered :

" Oh ! the details are far beneath Your Majesty's notice.   Just give them to me—that's all I ask."   He smiled, and very few people could resist Hugh's smile.   " Won't you be generous, Sire ? " he asked gently.   "It's not much to ask, and I've never asked you for anything before."

" Oh ! good gracious," cried the King, half angry, half amused.   " Take the wretched huts if you want them, and much good may they do you ! "

Hugh went back to Witham highly delighted, and soon there were others there even more delighted than he.

For word went round among the peasants.   There would be new land for all who had been dispossessed by the building of the monastery, with good money to help in starting life afresh, for the King had bought all their huts and the money he paid was to be divided between them. But not only that—they were to be allowed to pull down and take away with them the huts themselves. The King had given them to the new Prior, and he had given them back to the people.

" Didn't I say he looked a kindly soul ! " remarked the woman who had first told of Hugh's coming.

Then all day long the air rang with the sound of hammer and saw—the people of Witham were moving, and taking with them the little homes they loved. And they were taking something else, too. The knowledge that at last they had found a friend who understood their needs and would stand up for them.

" *Foreigner!* " scoffed the Oldest Inhabitant. " Don't 'ee talk silly. Prior Hugh be one of *us*."

That was how the people always felt about Hugh.

The peasants being now happily settled in a new place, the next thing to do was to build the monastery. The monks set to work, and with the help of those peasants who lived near enough they built the walls. Then they came to a stop.· There was no more money.

" His Majesty distinctly promised it," said an old monk. " Distinctly."

" Promised ! " snorted Brother Gerard of Nevers, a rather hot-tempered person. " Piecrust promises—that's what his are ! "

" We will send word to the King," said Hugh.

Off went some of the monks to King Henry. They returned quite cheerful. Yes, some money would come— the King had promised faithfully.

" When ? " demanded Brother Gerard.

" Soon. Quite soon."

But it did not come. At last they got tired of waiting. Another deputation went to the King. Back it came again —not quite so cheerful this time.

" Well ? Have you got the money ? " the others asked, eagerly.

" Well—er—" the deputation replied, " we haven't actually got it yet.   But he promised——"

And again they waited.   And still the money did not come.

At last Brother Gerard went to Hugh in a rage.

" Father Prior," said he, " how long are you going to stand this ?   You should go to the King yourself.   Go and tell him that we must have the money to finish the monastery.   Tell him that if he doesn't let us have it at once we will leave Witham and go back to where we came from. It's absurd going on like this, and if you don't go and tell the King—I will."

" Very well," said Hugh, " I will go.   And you had better come too."

" Gladly," said Brother Gerard. " Nothing will please me better than to give His Majesty a piece of my mind."

Hugh laid a hand gently on his shoulder.

" By all means speak the truth to the King," said he, " but when you do so, remember to speak it with love and patience, won't you ? "

So Hugh, Brother Gerard, and one other monk, set out to see the King.   His Majesty received them very politely and heard most graciously what Hugh had to say.

" Yes, yes," said he, when Hugh had finished, " of course you shall have the money.   I give you my word— my royal word.   The very first thing tomorrow I'll see about it.   Not at all—don't mention it—I'm glad you came to see me—good morning ! " and he graciously waved his hand to show that the interview was at an end.

But someone else thought otherwise. During the King's speech Brother Gerard had been getting more and more furious.   Now, without warning, he suddenly burst out :

" Listen, my Lord King. We've heard too many of your promises. They may be good enough for other people but they're not good enough for me, and so I tell you ! We should be better off at Grande Chartreuse, with all its hardships, than here, waiting for a King who is so mean that he can't bear to part with a penny ! Now, listen to me.   Either you give us the money *now*, or I, for one, will leave the place altogether and have nothing more to do with it ! "   He stopped at last, breathless, and stood glaring at the King.

For a moment you could have heard a pin drop.   Not a page, not a courtier moved.   All eyes were turned upon the King, who stood there, breathing quickly, his eyes flashing, his face crimson with anger.   What awful thing would befall the man who had dared to speak to him so ?

Only Hugh looked at the King with neither fear nor blame in his eyes.

Suddenly, the King spoke.   Looking at Hugh very intently, he said : " And you ? Will you also leave my Kingdom ? "

Hugh gave him back look for look, but his voice was quiet and friendly.

" No, my Lord King," he answered.   " I know you have a great many things to think of, and therefore you sometimes forget those which are most important.   I am sure you will do what you have promised."

Slowly, the angry colour faded from the King's face. Someone had trusted him : someone had *expected* him to do the right thing.   Because of that person—he would do it. There and then he sent for the money he had promised and gave it into Hugh's hands.

" Thank you, Sire," said Hugh, smiling at him.   Then, turning to Brother Gerard, he said, " Brother Gerard, will you take charge of this ? "

As the monks were leaving the Court, Henry drew Hugh aside.

" I want you," said he, " to be my adviser.   Oh ! not about state matters—I've got plenty to advise me about those.   But I—I would like you to guide me, so that I shall be a—a good Christian."

" Of course I will, Your Majesty," promised Hugh. " I hope you won't mind if I am rather stern sometimes ? "

" Not a bit," replied the King.   " I seem to be able to take anything from you."

" There you are, you see ! " said Brother Gerard triumphantly, as the monks set off again for Witham. " A bit of straight talking—that's all he wanted. You've got to know how to deal with people."

" Exactly," agreed the other monk. " As Father Hugh does."

Hugh merely smiled.

Now there was nothing to hinder the building of the monastery, and soon it was finished. No more huts made of twigs. The monks had a beautiful home of their own at last. Now that it was really finished, Hugh wanted to fill the monastery with everything that could help him and his monks to live well and truly in God's service. He was talking about this to the King one day. Since the time when he and the other two monks had gone to see him about the building money, Hugh and the King had become great friends.

" What I specially want," said Hugh, " is a complete copy of the scriptures. Of course we have the gospels separately, but I would give anything to have the whole Bible in one volume."

The King said nothing much at the time, but he made a mental note of it, and secretly made enquiries as to where such a thing could be found. Bibles were rare in those days. It was more usual to have the different parts bound up as separate books. Even the King could not be sure of getting one. At last, however, he learnt that there was a complete Bible at the monastery of St. Swithuns, Winchester. Thereupon, he sent for the Prior, and calmly told him he would like to have it ! That Bible was a great treasure, all handwritten by the monks themselves, and the Prior could hardly bear to part with it. But he was a nice kind of man, and, thinking that the King had done the monastery a great honour by his request, he gave the book up without any fuss.

The King was quite delighted, and, chuckling with pleasure at the thought of Hugh's surprise, he had the book sent off at once to Witham with his best wishes.

When Hugh opened the parcel and saw the beautiful Bible he could not speak for a moment, he was so pleased. At last he exclaimed :

" Just the very thing I wanted ! "

The monks were all delighted too, and crowded round, examining the treasure.

" Look, do you see ? " said one, " there is room for us to add our own illumination ?   Everyone can do a little. Oh ! we can make it the most beautiful book ! "

" His Majesty is most generous," said Hugh, lovingly stroking the covers of their new treasure.

Not one of them dreamed how the King had got it, nor that his generosity was at someone else's expense.   But that kind of secret has a funny way of coming out most un-expectedly.   One day, not long after this, a monk from Winchester happened to visit Witham.

" You haven't seen our latest treasure, have you, Brother ? " said one of the monks, proudly.   " See ! " He took up the Bible.   " His Majesty the King sent it to us himself."

The Winchester monk's eyes nearly jumped out of his head.   " But—but that's *our* Bible ! " he cried.

" Yours ! " said the other, " but it can't be ! His Majesty the King—— "

Just then Hugh appeared.   " What is the matter ? " he asked, looking from one to the other.

" He—he—he says— " spluttered the Witham monk, clasping the precious Bible to him with both arms—" He says it's his ! "

By this time the Winchester monk was feeling rather awkward.

" It doesn't matter," he protested hastily.   " You are quite welcome."

"One moment," said Hugh. " This must be cleared up. You say this Bible is yours, Brother ? "

" It belongs to our monastery," replied the monk. " You see, His Majesty asked our Prior to give it to him, so naturally he did so—though we did wonder a little.

However," he added politely, " I am very glad it has been put to such good use, and I'm sure our Prior will agree."

Hugh took the Bible, and turned it slowly over in his hands, smiling an odd little smile to himself. " Poor Henry," he thought, " he hasn't learnt the first thing about giving."

The Winchester monk was looking at him anxiously.

" Of course," he suggested, " I don't know if that copy *suits* you. It suited us perfectly, but then—I mean—in different monasteries— If you liked I could take it back and we would make you another. Then you could have it arranged to suit yourselves——"

Hugh looked up quickly. " You must take the Bible back at once," said he, " and please offer your Prior my most sincere apologies. Tell him I should never have dreamed of accepting it had I known—but I had not the slightest idea it was really yours."

But now the Winchester monk began to be scared.

" Oh! I don't think I'd better do that," he said. " I don't really. You see, if the King heard about it there might be trouble. In fact I'm sure there would be. Really, I'd rather you kept it. I'm sure our Prior——"

" I shall certainly not keep it," said Hugh, firmly.

The poor monk looked more and more terrified. " But the King ! " he wailed. " You know what he is ! "

Hugh was really very annoyed about the whole thing, but he could not help smiling.

" I do indeed," he said. " It's all right, Brother, I won't get you into trouble. Look—we won't tell the King anything about it. You just take the Bible back quietly and don't say a word to anyone, and he will never know."

When the monk got back to Winchester and showed what he had brought, the monks of St. Swithun were delighted, and from that time a great friendship sprung up between them and the monks of Witham.

Strangers and Friends

OME time later, a little group of horsemen were riding through the Somerset lanes towards the monastery at Witham. You could tell by their dress that they were Churchmen. As a matter of fact they were Canons of Lincoln Cathedral and they were bringing a message to Hugh. They looked rather glum, for they did not at all approve of the message they were carrying.

" I wonder what he'll say ? " remarked one.

" Say ! " exclaimed another. " What would you say if you were invited to be Bishop of Lincoln ? Yes please, of course ! "

The first Canon, a plump little man, sighed heavily.

" Oh, dear ! oh, dear ! It's going to be most difficult. They say he eats scarcely anything, and wears a hair shirt, and as for work—he simply never stops. Supposing he expects *us*——"

" You'll never survive a hair shirt, Brother," chuckled one of the other Canons. " Well, it's a bad business. What possessed the King I can't imagine."

The trouble was this. For some time there had been no Bishop of Lincoln. Consequently, things had got into rather a bad way there. The Cathedral was falling into ruins, and the Canons, not having a Bishop to look up to, had become rather slack and lazy. Suddenly, King Henry decided that a new Bishop should be appointed, so he sent for the Archbishop of Canterbury and the Canons of Lincoln Cathedral, to come to Eynsham, where he was staying, and hold a Council there with him to choose someone for the position. Each secretly hoping that he might be chosen, the Canons obeyed. To their astonishment, the King announced that he had decided that the new Bishop of Lincoln should be Hugh of Witham. The Canons were horrified. They had heard a lot about the strict life that Hugh led, and they were dreadfully afraid that he would expect them to do the same. However, the choice was the King's and the Archbishop confirmed it, so what could they do?

That was how it happened that a very disgruntled party of Canons was riding towards Witham.

But when they got there they had the surprise of their lives.

Instead of being thoroughly delighted at the high position offered him, Hugh said quietly:

" But that is not the way in which a Bishop should be chosen! It is the Canons of the Cathedral alone who must choose the Bishop, at a meeting held in the Chapter House. That is the law of the Church, as I think, Brothers, you very well know. Now, will you please go back to the King and say that I thank him and the Archbishop very much, but I cannot be Bishop of Lincoln unless I am chosen in the right way. Then hold your own meeting, in the Chapter House at Lincoln, and, first asking God to guide you, choose whom you think best for your Bishop."

The Canons rode soberly away. For many miles none of them spoke. At last the fat little one said slowly:

" He's quite different from what I expected."

" Not many people would refuse a position like that," said another, thoughtfully.

" It seems to me," announced a third Canon, boldly, " that he is just the very man we want. I—I shouldn't at all mind working *quite hard* if he were our Bishop, and I for one would vote——"

" Wait, Brother," said the first Canon. " This must be done in the proper way, as Father Hugh said."

Well, the Canons held their meeting, and perhaps you won't be very surprised to learn that they chose Hugh for Bishop. Even then, he insisted that he must first get permission from the Prior at Grande Chartreuse to leave Witham, but the Prior gave it readily and then everything was settled.

Hugh was sorry to leave Witham, and the monks there were sorrier still to lose him : so were the peasants living round about. So altogether no one was feeling very cheerful when, one fine morning, a gallant company gathered at the monastery gates to escort their new Bishop to London to be consecrated and then on to Lincoln· to be enthroned in his Cathedral. There were Canons, Clerks and Chaplains, attendants and serving men of all kinds. There were fine horses, sleek mules, mountains of luggage. In fact, it was a very grand company indeed. Everyone wore his best clothes : the harness of the horses sparkled with gold and silver : even the mules who carried the luggage had been specially groomed for the occasion.

" I hope," began the fat little Canon anxiously, " I do hope we have enough sumpter mules. I don't quite know how much luggage the Prior will——" He stopped. Hugh had just joined them.

He was wearing his old Carthusian monk's habit, and riding a mule with a plain, rather worn harness. Behind him was strapped the horsecloth and sheepskin which served him for bedclothes, rolled up into a rough bundle.

" He's never going to London like that ! " gasped the fat little Canon in a horrified whisper.

" Whatever's that tied on the back of his mule ? " whispered another.

" It must be his luggage," the fat one wailed. " I shall be ashamed to ride through the streets with him ! " He urged his horse nearer to Hugh. " Er—h'm ! " he began. " Shall I have your—your luggage put on one of the sumpter mules, Father ? "

Hugh glanced carelessly at his old bundle.

" No. No, that's all right," he replied cheerfully. " I always carry it like that."

" But—but I assure you," persisted the Canon, mopping his brow in an agitated way, " there are plenty——"

But Hugh was not listening. The party had begun to move off, and he was already lost to everything around him, for he was saying his prayers, and that was a thing he never did by halves. He always did ˎsay his prayers when he was riding, and once he began he so completely forgot everything else that someone had to be told off to keep an eye on him, for fear he should get lost, or tack himself on to another party without noticing. It was nothing, when Hugh was travelling, to meet a very hot and bothered servant galloping down the road, crying : " Goodness gracious, I've lost my Bishop ! "

However, they managed to get him safely to his journey's end this time, but as they drew near the city the Canons grew more and more agitated about his " luggage."

" Something has *got* to be done about that bundle ! " insisted one of them. " I will *not* be seen riding through the streets in the company of that bundle ! "

The fat little Canon came to the rescue. " Give me your knife," he whispered to a servant. Then, leaning forward, he gently cut the strings which tied the offending bundle. " Here, take it," he whispered, pushing it into the servant's arms. " Get rid of it somehow."

A sigh of relief echoed throughout the party. Hugh rode on, all unconscious.

On the day on which their new Bishop was to arrive, the people of Lincoln were up early, for they all wanted to see the procession. A fine affair it would be, with many great Churchmen, riding their finest horses and wearing their richest robes : with singing, and candles, and the Bishop——

" How shall we know which is the Bishop ? " enquired a small girl named Mary, who had come with her parents, and her brother John, to see the procession.

" *I* know," her brother told her, importantly. " He'll have the most *loveliest* robes of all, and he'll ride a great, big TREMENDOUS horse—won't he, Father ? "

"Hush!" said their mother, "the procession is coming."

Slowly the magnificent procession wound its way between the people. The crowd gazed in wonder at the bright robes, the jewels, the gold and silver ornaments.

Suddenly, the voice of the small girl rang out clearly:

"Oh! there's a poor man without any shoes and stockings on!"

The "poor man" must have heard, for he turned and gave her the sweetest smile.

She smiled back at him. "I like the 'poor man' best," she informed her brother. "You can have the Bishop."

"Hush!" whispered her father, horrified. "*That was the Bishop.*"

And so it was. He had spent the night at a Priory outside the city gates. From there, he walked barefoot all the way to the Cathedral.

The procession over, the crowd began to break up.

"Come along, Mary," said the small girl's mother, "and you too, John. We are going home to dinner."

"Where will the Bishop have his dinner?" enquired Mary.

"At his fine Manor of Stow, outside the city," her father explained. "That's where he will live now. Later on he will give a banquet there for all the great folk. With venison."

"Ooo!" sighed Mary. "I would like some venison."

"Silly," scoffed her brother. "Poor folk don't have venison. The Bishop won't give us any."

"Yes he will then," asserted Mary, firmly. "I'm sure he will. Father, how many deer will they——"

That was just what the steward at Stow wanted to know.

"How many deer shall I have killed for the banquet, my Lord Bishop?" he enquired.

Hugh considered.

"About three hundred, I should think," he said. "More, if you need them. I don't want anyone to go short—why, what's the matter?" for the steward was gaping at him as if he thought the new Bishop had gone out of his mind.

"But—but we don't need anything like that number, my Lord," he exclaimed. "Twenty would be ample for your guests."

"All the people of Lincoln are to be my guests, Steward," Hugh replied. "Rich or poor, they shall all eat venison this once at least."

"Venison! Venison!" shouted John, when the fine joint came to the table. "Doesn't it smell good!"

"I told you the Bishop would give us some," said Mary, in her most grown-up tone.

The people very soon discovered that their new Bishop would give them something much more than a nice dinner. He would give them love, justice, kindness, sympathy. The great ones of the world had always plenty of friends. Here, at last, was someone who would be a friend to them —the poor, the simple, the ignorant. Someone who would stand up for them—yes, even against the King himself if need be.

It was not long before they had proof of this. Those were the great days of hunting. The King and his nobles loved it above all things. What is more, they seemed to regard the whole of England as a great hunting park set out for their especial benefit. There were most cruel game laws, for breaking which a peasant could be punished terribly. In order that the King and his courtiers might enjoy a good day's hunting, farm labourers would often have to leave their fields and let the wild beasts feed upon their crops, shepherds must not lead their flocks to pasture. Never mind about feeding the people; about keeping the good English land well cultivated—the King must have his hunt. Foresters were there to see that these laws were obeyed and they could do practically what they liked to the people. No one can have such power without misusing it sooner or later, and the foresters soon developed into a regular band of tyrants.

M

From the first, Hugh fought against these men, and the cruel game laws, and it was not long before he came up against one man in particular.   This was a forester named Galfrid, who tormented and persecuted the tenants on the land so much that Hugh, after protesting again and again, at last excommunicated him.

King Henry was terribly angry at this, declaring that the man was his servant and should not have been punished without his permission.   However, he said nothing to Hugh at the time, but waited his chance to repay him.

Soon afterwards one of the Canons of Lincoln Cathedral died.   Thereupon, some of the King's men had what they thought was a brilliant idea.   " Let's ask the King," they said, " to write and tell Bishop Hugh to give one of us the position.   The Bishop knows the King was furious with him over that matter of the forester Galfrid, so he'll be only too glad to do something to oblige the King and get himself back into favour."

So they went and asked the King, and the King agreed, and sent a messenger to Hugh with a letter, just as the courtiers wanted.

Hugh looked very stern as he read it.   Then he said :

" Tell the King that the places in the Church are given to those who have served God well, in order that they may serve Him still better.   They are not to be handed out as favours for courtiers.   If His Majesty wishes to reward his subjects for anything they have done there are plenty of lands and honours he can give them himself."

Well ! that was the last straw.   The King was at Woodstock, near Oxford, at the time, while Hugh himself was at Dorchester (not the one in Dorset, but another place not far from Woodstock).

" Tell that—that—that *fellow* to come here at once ! " he commanded.   Messengers went galloping off to Hugh with the King's command.   " I wouldn't be in his shoes for anything," said one to another.

Meanwhile, the King had ordered his horse, and with a group of courtiers, rode off into the woods near by.

"What's the idea?" muttered the courtiers to each other, as they rode along. "Why are we going off like this when he's only just sent for the Bishop?"

They soon learned. Reaching a clearing in the wood, the King dismounted and seated himself on a fallen tree.

"Sit down, gentlemen," he said, "and listen to me. The Bishop of Lincoln will probably arrive here soon. When he comes, let no one rise, or greet him. Just ignore him completely. I mean to teach him a lesson."

The courtiers murmured agreement. Most of them were jealous of Hugh and were delighted at the thought of seeing him "put in his place," as they called it.

They had not been sitting there long when they saw him coming through the trees towards them. He had been very much surprised when he reached Woodstock and found the King out, and rather expected trouble. However, he did not hesitate, but came forward and greeted them in his usual polite and friendly way.

Nobody answered: nobody so much as looked at him. They all just sat staring stonily before them.

Hugh stood looking down at the little circle. His mouth was grave, but his eyes were dancing with mischief —they looked so like a group of sulky schoolboys. Then, gently pushing aside the man who sat next to Henry, he calmly sat down beside the King!

A kind of gasp went round the circle, but still nobody spoke.

And there they all sat for what seemed like ages. Some of the courtiers fiddled with their gloves or their belts: some chewed grass stems: some just stared at the ground. One of the younger ones began to giggle, and hastily turned it into a cough. The King sat looking as black as a thundercloud. Only Hugh did not seem at all uncomfortable. He had learned long ago, at Grande Chartreuse, how to be still and silent.

At last the silence began to get really awkward. Suddenly, the King turned to one of his attendants and asked for a needle and thread. He had cut his finger, and now, just for something to do, began to stitch a piece of linen round it. Stitch, stitch, he went, pretending to be absolutely engrossed in what he was doing.

All at once the silence was broken. Hugh spoke :

" How you do remind me of your great grandmother of Falaise, Sire ! " he remarked.

There really was a gasp this time. The courtiers simply did not know where to look, for everyone knew that the King's grandmother was a tradesman's daughter. They certainly expected him to order Hugh's arrest. Instead—he burst out laughing.

" I'm afraid you don't see the joke, gentlemen," he said to the astonished courtiers, as soon as he could speak. " The fact is, this impudent fellow "—he dug Hugh playfully in the ribs—" has just reminded me that my great grandmother was no high-born lady, but a glove maker in the town of Falaise."

Then he turned to Hugh, and demanded to know all about the affair of Galfrid, and when he really learned the details of the matter he agreed that Hugh was quite right in punishing him.

So that little trouble was over, and Hugh and the King were friends again. The funny thing is that Galfrid, too, ended by being one of Hugh's most faithful followers and friends.

But Hugh had friends everywhere, because he was always ready to be friendly and helpful himself. Especially he tried to help those who could not do much for themselves. First, there were the lepers. He built hospitals for them, and what was better still, he used to go himself to feed, nurse and comfort them. Then there were the Jews. Even in England there have been times when Jews were persecuted just for *being* Jews. But Hugh would have none of that when he was about, and once, when he came upon a crowd who were Jew baiting he rushed in among them and indignantly commanded them to stop.

As for children—Hugh simply loved them and they simply loved him, and when he went down the street all the babies held out their arms to come to him. As you can imagine, he had to travel about a lot, and he would often come upon a little group of children waiting by the roadside for him to pass.

You see, in those times churches were few and far between and often the country people just could not take their children to church to be confirmed. So they used to wait with them by the roadside along which the Bishop would be passing, and he would bless them when he came. Some proud and haughty Bishops would not bother to dismount, but hastily bless the children as they passed. Not Hugh, however. He never did important things in a hurry. As soon as he saw the children he would dismount, and bless them as lovingly as if he had come all the way to that spot for no other purpose. And woe betide anyone who hustled them or was rough with them ! Once, when one of Hugh's own servants treated the children so he turned and hit him—hard.

When Hugh first came to Lincoln, the Canons were afraid they were going to have a very rough time, but they soon found that they were wrong, for though he was awfully hard on himself, always wearing a hair shirt and simple monk's dress, eating no meat and very little of anything else, and working enough for three men, he never expected others to do the same.

He liked to see his household merry and bright, too. He himself was ever so jolly and full of fun, and though he was very serious over serious things, at a feast or a festival, he was the life and soul of the party. At mealtimes, you could always tell where Hugh was sitting because of the roars of laughter that came from that end of the table, and there was quite a competition to sit near him, in order to enjoy the fun.

When Hugh was made Bishop of Lincoln the Cathedral was falling into ruins. As soon as he had settled down, he began to rebuild it.

Building a Cathedral in those days was great fun. Everyone helped. Those who could carve or paint, make stained glass windows or do sculpture, were proud to offer their services. Those who could not do anything special sawed wood or carried stones or mixed mortar, pushing or pulling the heavy loads and singing all the time. In spite of all his other work, Hugh found time to join the workers. He did not care what he did, and it was nothing for the people of Lincoln to meet their Bishop carrying a great load of something for the building, like a common labourer. When at last it was finished it was one of the finest Cathedrals in England. There is one part called the Angel Choir, which is particularly beautiful.

Before we finish this part of the story I must tell you about another newcomer who arrived at Lincoln just about the same time as Hugh. Not a man—but a bird—an enormous Swan.

The servants found it on the lake in the park at Stow— the finest and largest Swan they had ever seen. Where it came from no one knew.

" My, what a creature ! " cried one of the servants. " I guess the Bishop would like to see it."

" Let's take it to him," suggested someone. So the Swan was caught, and carried to the Bishop's room.

" Why, what a splendid fellow ! " exclaimed Hugh. " Greeting, My Lord Swan. You and I must be friends, for we are both strangers here."

Evidently, the Swan agreed, for to the surprise of everyone, it was as tame as a pet canary with Hugh, and from that day would scarcely leave him. It would lie by his side while he worked, follow him about, indoors and out, eat from his hand, and even push its head right up inside his wide sleeves, muttering away in swan language as though it were talking to Hugh. At night it liked to lie by his bedside, and if anyone wanted to pass—well, they just couldn't, because the Swan would set up such a noise and such a beating of wings that it would waken its master.

When Hugh went away, the Swan retired to the lake, but at the first sign of his return it would begin to fly up and down, just above the surface of the water, squarking excitedly—then stride down to the front gate with a great air of importance, as much as to say, " Stand aside, please. I have to meet the Bishop ! " When Hugh finally arrived, the Swan would come stalking down the front steps, insisting upon being the first to greet him, then lead the way into the hall and up the stairs—" Squark ! Squark Out of the way—stand aside, please—the Bishop and I are here ! "

Swans can be fierce sometimes, and this one would let no one but Hugh come near it. Only when he was away it would graciously condescend to take its food from a servant.

For years it was Hugh's faithful friend. Then, suddenly, it seemed to fall ill. Instead of following Hugh everywhere it slunk away to a hidden part of the lake. Hoping he might be able to find out what was wrong, Hugh told the servants to catch it and bring it to him, but when it was at last brought it seemed hardly to know him. For a while it moped about, ill and miserable, and then it died.

Six months later, Hugh himself died. It seemed almost as if the Swan had known what was to happen, and had itself died of grief for its master.

Hugh Goes Home

BUT before this came about a great many things were to happen to Hugh and to England. To begin with, Henry II died, and Richard I—Richard the Lion Heart—became King of England. As you know, he was a great one for Crusades, and what with these and war with France, he soon began to want some money. He was casting about for a way to get some when one of his nobles had a bright idea.

" What about the sable mantle from Lincoln, Your Majesty ? " he suggested.

" What sable mantle ? " demanded the King.

The nobleman explained. Did not the King remember that it was the custom for a Bishop of Lincoln to send to the King a mantle of fine sables or 100 Marks ?

" Why, of course ! " cried the King. " Haven't we had it yet ? Let a messenger go to Bishop Hugh at once and demand a mantle of sables or—— No ! better say definitely the hundred Marks. There might be something wrong with the furs. You know where you are with money."

" And you might claim another hundred as a fine for not having paid before," suggested the wily nobleman.

" That's a bright idea ! " exclaimed the King. " One hundred Marks, and another hundred for a fine. Can't have these good old customs dying out, you know ! "

Hugh knew all about the mantle of sables. He had not sent one because he thought the money should be spent on the Church and people of Lincoln and not upon the King. However, he did not want to quarrel about it : beside, he thought he saw a way of ending that old custom altogether. So, when the messenger arrived he sent him back with a message offering to pay not one hundred Marks, but three thousand, on condition that neither mantle nor money should ever be asked of a Bishop of Lincoln again, and the King, highly delighted, agreed.

The Canons of Lincoln, however, were in a great state

of mind over it. "But where is the money to come from?" they protested.

"Oh! I've got a fine idea about that," Hugh told them. "Listen—I'll go into retreat at Witham, and while I'm there all the money I should have spent here at Lincoln can be saved up for the King. We shall soon get enough that way. Eh? What's the matter? Don't you like the idea?"

The Canons definitely did not. The idea of doing without their Bishop for weeks and months did not appeal to them at all. So they put their heads together and devised a better way still. They would collect the money themselves, they announced.

"Well—that's awfully good of you," said Hugh. "Of course, if you'd rather do it that way—— Only, everyone must give of their own free will, mind. Nobody must be *made* to give. Promise!"

The Canons promised faithfully, and that was how the three thousand Marks were collected. The Canons felt very pleased at the success of their plan.

But Hugh sighed a little to himself. He had looked forward to going to Witham.

War is very expensive. It is like pouring little pails of water into parched soil, to spend money on war. The three thousand Marks were gone in no time. Richard, who was in France with his army, sent home to say—" Send me some more money, quickly!"

There was not any money to send, so a meeting of Barons and Bishops was called to see what could be done about it. The Archbishop of Canterbury suggested that each Baron and Bishop should raise a force of three hundred knights to fight for the King, which would be as good as sending the money, if not better. The Barons agreed, and so did most of the Bishops, but when it came to Hugh's turn, he refused. He would not, he said, spend money drawn from English folk and English land to fight foreign wars. They would get no three hundred knights from him. Thereupon, the Bishop of Salisbury stood up and said he would not agree either, and in the end the Council broke up without deciding anything. The Archbishop had to send word to the King that it had failed. It was, he said, entirely the fault of the Bishop of Lincoln, who refused to do his share.

The King was frightfully angry, and gave orders that Hugh was to be disgraced, and his property taken from him. But no one wanted to carry the order out. Some refused because they loved Hugh too much, some because they feared him. At last some men were found to do what the King commanded, but when they reached Lincoln, instead of setting about it, they fell on their knees before Hugh and begged him to go himself and pacify the King.

" I ! " exclaimed Hugh, pretending to be very much surprised. " But I thought I was the culprit ! "

" Yes, my Lord ! No, my Lord ! " stammered the men. " He'll take notice of you, my Lord."

" Very well," said Hugh, " I'll go."

The King was actually in church, at a place called Andely, when he arrived. There he sat, on a kind of throne, with his nobles around him, while the Archbishop, at the other end, was ready to begin the service. As Hugh came into the church the King gave him a quick look— then looked away. Hugh stopped in front of him. I think he must have remembered the time when he had gone to see King Henry at Woodstock.

" Give me the kiss of peace, my Lord King," said he.

The King did not answer.

But Hugh knew all about how to treat kings who behave like sulky schoolboys. He caught hold of the King's cloak and gave it a little pull.

" I've come a long way, my son," he said gently. " I think I have a right to claim the salute."

" You don't deserve it," muttered the King, still not looking at him.

" Oh ! but I do," protested Hugh. " Come along now, pay me what you owe ! "

Then, to the horror and astonishment of the courtiers,

he took a firmer grip on the King's cloak and gave him a real good shaking.

It was just the same as at Woodstock. Instead of being angry, the King simply had to smile, and then everything was all right. The courtiers breathed a sigh of relief, and one of them who was sitting near Richard moved to make room for Hugh. But Hugh did not sit down beside the King this time. Shaking his head, he passed on to the altar, and kneeling there, soon forgot the very existence of Richard I of England.

But Richard did not forget him. The King's face was very thoughtful as the service went on, and when it came to an end he gave Hugh his kiss of peace with the greatest respect.

" If all Bishops were like him," said he, looking intently at Hugh, " no King would dare do wrong."

Unfortunately, the King's good mood did not last very long, and later, when Hugh would not agree to let some of his Canons act as Ambassadors for him, he again ordered Hugh's property to be taken. But before the order could be carried out, King Richard himself died.

And now there came to the throne one of the worst of all English Kings—King John. Hugh and King Henry had been real friends : King Richard he could get on with : but John—even Hugh, who was so patient and sympathetic with everyone—even he found King John hopeless.

At first the new King made a great pretence of being wonderfully good, but almost at once he gave himself away.

It was at church, and Hugh was holding the service. When collection time came, it was the custom for a court official to hand the King some gold pieces, which he would then give to the Bishop. John received the coins as usual, but instead of handing them to Hugh properly, he just stood carelessly chinking them together in his hand.

" Well ? What are you about ? " asked Hugh, sharply.

" I was thinking," said John, " that if I hadn't been King I could have kept these gold pieces for myself.

However—here you are——" and he went to push them roughly into Hugh's hand.

Hugh's eyes flashed : he stepped back.   Then, pointing to the offertory bowl :

" Drop them in there, and be off ! " he said, and turned away.

John's reign was a bad time for England, but people like Hugh helped to prevent things from getting too terrible.   In those days Bishops held courts in which they tried cases which would be tried in the Law Courts nowadays.   Hugh always had more cases than he could manage, because everyone wanted to be tried by him.   They knew he would give them fair play, no matter how poor and unimportant they were.

Hugh was awfully kind—especially to children—but even they could not play any tricks with him.   There was a boy named Martin who discovered that.

Martin was a sacristan at Lincoln Cathedral, and he had beautiful long golden curls.   And Martin was terribly proud of them.   In these days we should think a boy a great baby if he were proud of his curls—in fact most boys do their best to get rid of them if they happen to have any. But in Hugh's time long curly hair was quite the fashion for men, so nobody despised him for it.   A Churchman, however, always wore his hair short, and as you know, the monks have it shaved in what is called a tonsure.   So Martin should have had his cut.   Indeed, he kept meaning to, but they were such lovely curls—and—well, he didn't.

He hoped the Bishop would not notice, but the Bishop, being Hugh, did.

" Martin, you must have your hair cut," he said quietly, one day.

" Yes, my Lord Bishop," murmured Martin, but still he didn't.

Hugh gave him a little longer.   Then, one day, after the service, he and the boy were together in the vestry.

Suddenly, Hugh said ;

" Poor Martin, I see you haven't been able to find a barber yet. Come along, I'll do the job for you."

Then, picking up a pair of scissors, he took Martin's curls firmly in his hand, and then and there cut them off !

Before he had finished, Martin was crying, with his head in Hugh's lap.

" Oh ! I wanted to do it," he sobbed. " I did try, but somehow I—I couldn't. And I know God has called me to be a monk, but I—I couldn't listen properly because of the curls—and now I can ! "

" Wait a minute, Martin," said Hugh gently. " To be a monk is a very serious thing. You must think well and pray hard, and be perfectly certain before you start."

Martin promised to do so, and Hugh took great pains to help him. When they were both quite sure, he was sent to Normandy, where he lived and died a very good monk.

Now, all the time that Hugh lived in England, he never forgot the Grande Chartreuse. He always felt it was his real home, and he would gladly have gone back there to live, and given up all the glory of being a great Bishop to be a simple Carthusian monk again. Sometimes he used to go to Witham and live there just like one of the other monks. It was the next best thing, but—it wasn't Grande Chartreuse.

At last came a chance to go there, for a little holiday. He was called to France on some business, and having got so far he decided to go on to visit his old home.

All the way there it was quite a triumphal procession. His fame had spread all over the Continent and people came to greet him in great crowds at every point. At Grenoble the whole town turned out, the streets were decorated, and he preached to a huge crowd in the Cathedral.

Better still, both his brothers were there to welcome him, but what he liked best of all was baptising his little nephew, his brother William's son.

Leaving Grenoble, he went on again, and at last came to his beloved Grande Chartreuse. There he spent a wonderful three weeks, visiting all his favourite places, meeting all his old friends, and having the time of his life. Then he spent a little while at his home at Avalon, with William and Peter, and his little nephew. From there he visited Villarbenoit, and even little St. Maximin was not left out. It was the happiest time he had ever had, and though he did not know it, it was almost the end of his life. It is nice to think that it had such a happy ending.

It was at St. Omer, on his way back to England, that Hugh suddenly felt terribly tired and ill. He decided to stay there a few days before crossing to England, and after a rest he felt better. But, by the time he got to Dover, he was feeling very ill again, and could only get by short stages as far as London.

He lay at his house in the Old Temple, London, and by this time it was clear that he was dying. He lay there some months, and all manner of people came to see him. Most of them came, of course, for love of him, but there were some greedy Churchmen who came with a very different purpose. They had an idea that Hugh might leave them some money.

" Don't you think, my Lord Bishop," they suggested, " that you ought to make your will ? "

Hugh frowned. " I don't believe in wills," he said. " All that I have belongs not to me, but the Church. However, I shouldn't like there to be any quarrels over it. So, listen—I hereby leave all I have to the poor." Then he sent for his stole, and putting it on, he laid a solemn curse on anyone who should rob the poor of what he had left them.

The greedy Churchmen crept out—quite crestfallen. I hope they felt ashamed of themselves.

When Hugh felt the time was really getting near when he should die, he gave his last instructions.

" Bury me in my Cathedral," he said, " but lay me near the wall. Do not put my tomb right out in the middle of the pavement for careless people to tumble over."

" And now," he went on, " get some ashes that have been blessed in church, and when you see that it is time, spread them on the floor of my room in the shape of a cross. Next send for eight monks from the Westminster Choir. Then lay me on the cross of ashes, to remind me of Our Lord on His Cross, and let the choir sing Compline for me."

And so it was done. On the 16th November, 1200, lying on his cross of ashes, great Hugh of Lincoln died.

All England mourned for him. His coffin was carried from London to Lincoln, followed by a great procession. At every town and village that it passed, large crowds, especially of poor people, came to say good-bye to him.

At the Cathedral he was met by two kings—King John, and the King of Scotland. King John and three Archbishops carried his coffin to the altar.

Hugh's bones lie under the pavement of Lincoln Cathedral. The golden shrine which held his coffin has long since been destroyed. But all Lincoln Cathedral is his shrine: it is not too large for so splendid a Saint.

XIII

SAINT RICHARD OF CHICHESTER

The Younger Son

ICHARD DE WYCHE was a country boy. He and his brother Robert were the sons of a Squire, and they lived at a place called Wyche, in Worcestershire. It was a village then : now it is a town, called Droitwich.

Richard was the younger of the two boys. (He was born in 1197.) Sometimes a younger son is rather spoilt, but he wasn't. Far from it, as you shall hear.

While both boys were still quite young, their parents died. Robert, of course, inherited his father's Estate, but as he was not old enough to look after it, he had a Guardian to do it for him. Unluckily, the Guardian's idea was to look after himself, and bother the Estate ! Plenty to eat and drink, plenty of money to spend (out of Robert's inheritance), that was all he cared about. So things went from bad to worse. Young Robert was an easy going youth and troubled no more than his Guardian. Richard, who loved study, was always deep in his books. Now and then, he did feel a little anxious, but when he ventured to suggest that the land did not look too prosperous, the Guardian only answered :

" Now, you leave it to me, my boy. There's nothing to worry about. You get on with your lessons and leave everything to me."

Richard, only too glad to persuade himself that there

Richard worked like a common labourer.

was nothing wrong, buried himself in his beloved books once more.

But when Robert came of age, and the Guardian handed things over to him, both brothers had a shock. Because there was practically nothing to hand over.

" All in the land, my boy," said the Guardian airily. " All gone into the land. Absolutely eats money—the land does. But don't you worry—everything will be all right. Absolutely all right ! Well, I must be off—best of luck, Robert, my boy ! " and away he went—completely satisfied with himself.

The brothers were left gazing blankly at each other.

" All in the land ! " burst out Richard, indignantly. " Anyone would think he had buried Father's money in the garden, and all we had to do was just to dig when we wanted any."

Robert collapsed into a heap in the nearest chair.

" Whatever shall we do ? " he wailed. " We shall starve ! I know we shall ! "

"Nonsense ! " said Richard, briskly. "It's true the whole place has gone to rack and ruin, but we must just set to and put things right ourselves. After all, there *is* the land."

" But I can't. I don't know how ! " protested Robert. " Oh ! I *know* we're ruined."

Richard frowned. " For goodness sake, Robert," said he, " don't be so helpless and hopeless. Look here—let's ride round the Estate now and have a good look at it. We'll make a list of everything that needs doing, and then get to work upon it. Come on ! "

Robert hesitated. " I think my horse wants a shoe," he said doubtfully, " and I'm sure it's going to rain."

Richard drew in his breath sharply. " Oh ! don't be so——" helpless and hopeless, he was going to say, but he stopped himself. " It's no use," he thought, " he can't help it." Aloud, he said, " All right, I'll go by myself. I can manage quite well."

" Better," he added to himself, as he ran to fetch his horse.

The sights that greeted him as he rode round his brother's land that afternoon were not encouraging. Fences broken, fields uncultivated, cattle straying, cottages falling to pieces. " I ought to have noticed it before," he told himself. " I suppose I was too keen on studying to bother. Well—I shall have to leave books for a while and take to spades." He sighed. " Oh! well, *somebody's* got to."

From that day Richard worked like a common labourer on his brother's land—or rather, like an *un*common labourer. For beside doing all the hard and humble work —ploughing, digging, mending walls, milking cows, he planned the crops, kept the accounts, and generally played the part both of master and man. Robert helped, but it was Richard who was the leader. Soon the crops began to improve, the cattle to grow sleeker. They could afford some help on the farm. Richard's hard work and good management had saved the family fortunes. Once more there was a fine, well cared for Estate and plenty of money.

" It's all through you, Richard, really," said Robert, gratefully. " I don't know what I should have done without you."

He was so pleased that he planned a surprise for his brother. One morning, when Richard came to breakfast, he found a large folded parchment beside his plate.

" What's this ? " he asked, picking it up and eyeing it suspiciously.

" That's for you," said Robert, beaming at him. " The Title Deeds of the Estate. I want you to have it."

" I ? " said Richard, dropping the parchment like a hot coal. " Nonsense. You are the heir. The Estate is yours, of course."

" But I want you to have it," Robert insisted. " For all you've done. I'll make it over to you properly by law, of course——"

" I don't want it," said Richard shortly, getting on with his breakfast.

" But you *must* have it," urged Robert. " You deserve

it.   If it hadn't been for you there wouldn't *be* any Estate by now.   Do have it, Richard," he coaxed.   " I can't bear to feel that you've done all the work and I've got all the benefit.   Beside," he added, " I couldn't possibly look after it myself."

" All right," said Richard, after a pause.   " If you really mean it.   But if ever you want it back, let me know."

" Oh !   I should never take it back again ! " exclaimed Richard.   " That *would* be mean."

Now that Richard was a rich and successful young man, some of his relations began to take an interest in his future.

" You ought to get married, Richard," they said.

" I'm quite all right as I am, thanks," said Richard, hastily.

But the relations were not to be put off.   Marry, he must, they decided, and they did not rest until they had found a beautiful young girl to be his bride.

" Now it's all settled, Richard," said his eldest aunt, " so please don't be awkward.   The bride is chosen.   You have nothing to do but be charming to her.   We will arrange everything else."

" But I don't wish to marry," protested Richard.

" Nonsense," said his aunt.   " A rich young man like you must marry.   It is his duty."

" But you see——" began Richard.   Then gave it up in despair.

When Robert heard about it, he was rather jealous.

" What about me ? " he demanded of his brother. " Nobody takes the least interest in me now.   It's not fair. After all, I am Father's heir.   The Estate is mine really. Of course," he added hastily, " I know I gave it to you, Richard—and it's quite all right.   Only it is mine *really*, isn't it ? "

Richard looked at him narrowly.

" Do you want it back ? " he asked.

" No—Oh ! no," protested Robert, awkwardly.   " No, of course not.   I—I only meant——"

"Don't fret," said Richard, crisply. "You shall have it."

" Oh ! but I couldn't take it ! " exclaimed Robert.   " It would be dreadfully mean.   No, I couldn't really——"

" Yes, you could," said Richard, firmly.   " I will treat you as well as you treated me.   I will restore the whole thing to you."

" But—but—" protested Robert feebly, " it seems so mean."

" Nonsense," said Richard.   " The place is yours.   Is that agreed ? "

" Well—if you're quite sure."

" Of course I'm sure.   Shake hands on it."

They shook.

" You can have the beauteous bride as well if you like," offered Richard, handsomely.

" And pray," demanded the eldest aunt, when she heard of this arrangement, " pray, what might you be going to do, Richard ? "

" Me ? " replied Richard, cheerfully. " I'm going to Oxford."

Trouble with the King

RICHARD went off to Oxford with scarcely a penny in his pocket, and there he spent the happiest years of his life. He shared a room with two other young students. They were so poor that they could not afford meat but lived on bread and porridge. When it was cold they could not afford a fire, but ran about to keep themselves warm. As for clothes—they had only one gown between them, and this was the only part of being poor that they really minded, because it meant that they had to take it in turns to go to lectures.

But nobody cared whether you were rich or poor, high or low, in Oxford. Richard met all sorts of interesting and important people there, among whom was Edmund Rich, Chancellor of the University. Though Richard was only a poor student, and Edmund Rich was head of the whole University, they struck up a friendship which lasted for the rest of their lives.

Having learnt as much as he could at Oxford, Richard next went to Paris for more study, but he came back to Oxford to sit for his Master of Arts Degree, which he passed. Then, with M.A. after his name, he went abroad again to Bologna, where there was one of the best colleges in Europe. He did well there, and took another degree. Then something happened which was a little awkward.

Everyone at Bologna thought a great deal of Richard. Beside liking him, they could see that he was extremely clever, and would probably be a great man some day. In fact, one of his tutors felt so sure of this that he thought it would be a good idea if Richard were to be one of his family. This was where the awkwardness came in.

" Oh ! Richard," said the tutor one day, " can you spare a few minutes ? I should like a little chat with you. Sit down, won't you ? Well, now what I wanted to say was this. As you know, I have no son and heir. But I have a daughter, a good, beautiful and intelligent girl. My suggestion is that you should marry her, and I will make you my heir.   Well, what do you say ? ”

Poor Richard !   He swallowed hard : stood up : adjusted his gown : swallowed again, and said :

“ It’s—it’s extremely generous of you, Sir——”

“ Not at all !   Not at all ! ” interrupted the tutor, graciously.

Richard tried again.

“ It is extremely kind of you, Sir,” he said, with grave politeness, “ but—but you see, Sir, I don’t mean to marry at all.”

“ You don’t ! ” exclaimed the tutor, blankly.

“ No,” said Richard.   “ So you see, Sir, I am very much obliged to you, but I must say : ‘ No, thank you ’.”

“ Oh ! very well,” replied the tutor, in a disappointed tone.   “Of course, if you feel like that we will say no more.”

“ I do wish,” sighed Richard to himself, when he was safely outside the house, “ I do wish people wouldn’t keep on wanting to marry me to someone.   I think I shall go back to Oxford.”

At Oxford Richard settled down again very happily for a time.   His friend Edmund Rich had left and was now Archbishop of Canterbury, but he was well known and had plenty of friends.   Indeed there were many people watching his career with interest, for they, like the people at Bologna, felt sure he was going to do great things.

It soon began to seem that they were right.   First, he was chosen to be Chancellor of the University.   Not long afterwards he had two more offers of high and interesting positions.   The Archbishop of Canterbury and the Bishop of Lincoln both asked him to be their Chancellor.   He chose Canterbury (very likely because the Archbishop was his friend).   As Chancellor of Canterbury he had to act as a kind of assistant to the Archbishop, especially in judging people who had broken a law of the Church.   The same good points in his character which had enabled him to save his brother’s Estate, were valuable now, and he was a great success in his new position.

It was a difficult time just then, for there was trouble between the heads of the Church and the King. Richard I was dead and Henry III was the King of England and he was not behaving at all rightly. When a Bishop or anyone in a good position in the Church died or retired, instead of choosing a new one, Henry either left that place vacant and took the money that should have gone to the new Bishop, or put into the position some friend or relation of his own. Someone who neither knew or cared about the Church but who might be useful to him. The Archbishop of Canterbury had protested again and again, but it was hopeless, the King took no notice. It was just at this time that Richard came to be Chancellor of Canterbury, and through all his struggles with the King, he stood by his friend most loyally.

At last things got so bad that the Archbishop gave up in despair.   He was ill and he felt he could fight no longer. He decided to retire to a monastery at Pontigny in France.

" Then I shall come with you," announced Richard.

" No, no," said the Archbishop, " that is not necessary."

" But you can't possibly go off there alone with no one to look after you," protested Richard. " Please don't argue—I've made up my mind. I'm coming whether you want me or not."

" There is no question about wanting you," said the Archbishop gratefully.

So the two friends set off for France together, and Richard nursed the Archbishop there until he died.

After the Archbishop's death, Richard went to Orleans, where he spent another two years in study, and during that time he was ordained priest by the Bishop of Orleans. Then once more he returned to England.

He arrived in Deal and for a little while he worked there as an ordinary parish priest, but he was too clever and capable a person to be left in such a humble position long. He was soon recalled to Canterbury, by the new Archbishop, Boniface of Savoy, to take up again his work as Chancellor.

Now came the time when Richard himself came up against the King. The Bishop of Chichester died, and King Henry managed to get a man named Robert Passelowe elected in his place. He was a quite impossible person, not fit to be a clergyman at all—let alone a Bishop. The Archbishop of Canterbury therefore refused to confirm the election, and called a meeting to choose another man for the position.

The meeting chose Richard to be the new Bishop.

The King was furious. " He'll get nothing but the name then ! " he cried.

He would not allow Richard to have any of the land and money which belonged by right to the Bishop of Chichester. He just would not own that he *was* Bishop of Chichester.

Richard went himself to see the King about it : the King would not hear a word. He tried again : still the King would not listen.

" Very well," said Richard, " I shall go and see the Pope," and off he went to Rome.

The Pope said he was quite right, and wrote a letter about it for Richard to show to the King. Then he himself made Richard a Bishop.

Richard came back to England triumphant. He was already a Bishop—and he was quite determined to be Bishop of Chichester.

But the King had no intention of giving in. Richard came back to find the gates of the Bishop's Palace at Chichester barred against him. He had no home, and the King had forbidden anyone to shelter him : he had no money, and the King had forbidden anyone to lend him any.

Once more, Richard went to see the King.

He argued, he showed the Pope's own letter. Henry only raged and stormed, called him all kinds of names, and had him driven from the palace.

Richard set off for Chichester, wondering what to do next. He was without home : without money.

But not without friends. As he came near Tarring,

which is a village in Sussex, he met a man named Simon, Rector of Tarring.

" Good-day, my Lord Bishop," said the Rector. " It is a pleasure to see you home again."

" Is it ? " said Richard, smiling rather ruefully. " The King does not seem to think so."

The Rector pursed his lips. " I should wish always to remain a loyal subject of His Majesty," he said primly, " but when it comes to locking a Bishop out of his own Palace, no, that I can not approve ! "

" Neither can I," agreed Richard, heartily. " I'm beginning to wonder where I shall sleep tonight."

The Rector turned quite pink with excitement. " If your Lordship would honour me," he said, " my house is quite near. It is simple, but roomy, and you would be most welcome. *Most* welcome."

" Thank you," said Richard. " If you don't mind risking the King's displeasure, I will gladly come."

Richard stayed with Simon of Tarring for two years, doing his work from there. Cheerful and patient in spite of all the hardships and difficulties, he tramped about on foot, or on a borrowed horse, more like a missionary than a Bishop.

Then the Pope put his foot down. He ordered King Henry to restore Richard's property to him by a certain day without fail, or be excommunicated. That was more than even the King dared risk. With a very bad grace he gave in. At last he accepted Richard as Bishop of Chichester. The Bishop's Palace, with all the land and property belonging to it, were handed over to him.

Chichester at Last

UT when he came to take possession of them, Richard found everything poor, neglected and half in ruins.

"Dear me," said he, "History *does* repeat itself! This reminds me of brother Robert's Estate, after our Guardian had been 'looking after' it. Well, Robert and I put that in order. Let us see if we cannot do the same with this."

The first thing he did was to send for his brother Robert and make him Steward of his new property. Then, leaving Robert to put this in order, he set to work to do all he could to help anyone on his lands who was in trouble, and to repay all those who had helped him in his own hard times, by helping them in theirs. He did so much, and was so generous, that at last Robert protested.

"You really mustn't give so much away, Richard," he said. "You simply can't afford it. You don't seem to realise that it costs quite a lot to keep up the Palace alone. After all, now that you really are a Bishop, you can't just live anyhow. Things must be done in style!"

Richard laughed. Then he said gently :

"Robert, my dear, it will never do for us to eat out of gold and silver plates and bowls whilst other people are so poor (for you know that Our Lord suffers with them). Our father ate and drank heartily out of common crockery, and so can I."

"Yes, but——" began Robert.

"Sell the gold plate," said Richard. "That should fetch quite a good price. Oh! and my horse—better sell him, too."

"You are absolutely impossible!" sighed Robert, in despair.

That shows you something of what Richard was like.

Though he now had a palace to live in and servants to wait on him, he still lived most simply—more like a monk than a great Bishop. He was very hospitable—always having people to visit him, but though he gave them nice things to eat, he himself kept to the plainest food, and never ate meat.

He was most considerate for others, too. For instance, he always got up very early to go to church. On his way there, he had to pass through a dormitory where his clergy slept. They ought to have been up, and on their way to church like him, but sometimes they were so tired that they were still asleep when he passed through. Then Richard, instead of waking them, would leave them to have their sleep out, while he went on to church alone, and held the service himself.

He could be very stern with anyone who had done anything really wrong, but he could not bear that there should be quarrels among his people about land or money or things of that kind. " Those things," he would say, " must never divide friends.   They are just not important."

Richard was nine years Bishop of Chichester. When he was about fifty-five, he was chosen by the Pope to travel through England preaching to persuade people to go on a new Crusade.

He began at Chichester and then went on to Dover. There he stayed at a hostel for poor priests called the Hostel Dieu. After spending one night there he got up, just as usual, went to the chapel, and sang matins. But as he was standing, hearing Mass, he suddenly fell down in a kind of fit.

He was carried to the hospital and put to bed. As soon as he came to himself, he sent for his Chaplain.

" You know," he said to him, " I shan't get up again, I feel sure. Don't tell anyone, but just prepare secretly for my funeral."

He died soon afterwards and was buried in Chichester Cathedral, and though, after a while, his shrine was destroyed, there is still a chapel there dedicated to him, with pictures telling the story of his life.   It used to be a great place for pilgrims—Saint Richard's shrine, and for a long time the Cathedral was even called Saint Richard's Church.   It seems that the people remembered him very well.